This Time with Feeling

This Time with Feeling

Reimagining the Experience of Worship:
Creating the Space for Personal and
Communal Transformation

Susan Tarolli

WIPF & STOCK · Eugene, Oregon

THIS TIME WITH FEELING
Reimagining the Experience of Worship: Creating the Space for Personal and Communal Transformation

Copyright © 2021 Susan Tarolli. All rights reserved. Except for brief quotations in critical publications or reviews, no part of this book may be reproduced in any manner without prior written permission from the publisher. Write: Permissions, Wipf and Stock Publishers, 199 W. 8th Ave., Suite 3, Eugene, OR 97401.

Wipf & Stock
An Imprint of Wipf and Stock Publishers
199 W. 8th Ave., Suite 3
Eugene, OR 97401

www.wipfandstock.com

PAPERBACK ISBN: 978-1-6667-0402-0
HARDCOVER ISBN: 978-1-6667-0403-7
EBOOK ISBN: 978-1-6667-0404-4

09/01/21

Scripture quotations are from the New Revised Standard Version Bible (NRSV), copyright © 1989 by National Council of the Churches of Christ in the United States of America. Used by permission. All rights reserved worldwide.

The work "The Day Peter Ran," by Dr. Wilson of Joyful Heart Ministries, is used in this book, and he has been informed about this use, as per his request.

"If I Had Been," copyright © 1992 by Belwin-Mills Publishing Corp. All rights assigned to and controlled by Jubilate Music Group, LLC. All Rights Reserved. Used by Permission. www.jubilatemusic.com.

Édouard Manet, *Fish (Still Life)*, 1864, oil, 73.5 x 92.4 cm, Art Institute of Chicago. This information, which is available on the object page for each work, is also made available under Creative Commons Zero (CCO).

Contents

Gratitude | vii

Call to Worship | 1
    A Loss of Connection | 1
    Repurposing Christian Experience through Generations | 2
    Making the Faith Our Own in Worship | 4
    Reclaiming the Emotional Experience of Transformative Worship | 6
    Attending to Our Focus as Worship Planners | 7

1. Attending to Worship as an Emotional Experience | 9
    Getting Distracted | 10
    Educating and Advocating | 11
    Harboring Ulterior Motives | 11
    Misappropriating Ministry with Children | 12
    Adjusting the Focus of Worship Planning and Leadership | 13
    Creating Primary Theologians | 18

2. Attending to the Language of Worship: Words | 21
    The Blessing and Limitation of Age-Old Refrains | 22
    The Blessing and Limitation of Biblical Images | 25
    The Blessing and Limitation of Theological Terms | 29
    The Blessing and Limitation of Borrowed Words | 34
    Maintaining the Connection to the Essential Gospel | 40

3. Attending to the Language of Worship: Music | 42
    Musical Offerings | 42
    A Valuable Link between Science and Faith Experience | 45
    Music as Distraction | 50
    Musicians as Worship Leaders | 51

4. Attending to the Language of Worship: Symbols and Ritual | 55
    Symbols as Definition of Sacred Space | 56
    Discovering the Unintended Markers of Sacred Space | 57
    Symbols as the Artwork of Belief | 61
    Open to Interpretation | 63
    Symbols as Windows to Seeing God | 67
    Rituals | 70

5. Attending to the Story | 76
    The Liturgical Calendar: Gathering Together, Telling Stories, and Marking Time | 77
    Biblical Story as Compass | 78
    Reclaiming Ritual | 79
    Reimagining the Advent Experience | 81
    Inhabiting the Bible Story | 85
    Becoming the Storytellers of Holy Week | 87
    A Living Proclamation | 90

6. Attending to the Emotional Flow of Worship | 91
    Syncing Liturgical Elements with the Emotional Flow of Worship | 92
    Liturgical Mapping | 95

7. Attending to Virtual Worship | 98
    Liberation from Fear and Unknowing | 99
    Defining the Worship Space | 99
    Attending to the Language of Virtual Worship | 101
    Creating the Space for Epiphanies in Virtual Worship | 104
    Looking Forward | 106

Benediction | 111

Appendix 1: Reimagining Psalm 23 in the Context of an Infant's Baptism | 115
Appendix 2: Centering Ourselves in the Generosity and Forgiveness of God | 116
Appendix 3: Prayers for End-of-Life Services | 118
Appendix 4: Advent Candle-Lighting Liturgy | 121
Appendix 5: Worshippers Participating in the Drama of Jesus' Last Days | 126

Bibliography | 133
Index | 135

Gratitude

A MOOSE. WHEN I consider the graces that have led to the publication of this book, my gratitude begins with the God who made the moose I encountered at Rock Springs Guest Ranch in Bend, Oregon, decades ago. I sensed a call to step away from the law degree I was pursuing, and my dear friend and disciple of Christ, Krista Davis Bothman, welcomed me to the ranch where she was working—a lush, green, peaceful, alive space that played host to one of the most transformative moments of my life. Taking a solitary walk on wooded trails, I came face to face with a moose. When I returned to the main campus, I sat down on a grassy knoll, and began a conversation with God that was the beginning of a deeper personal relationship with the Divine than I had ever known. To God, the moose, Krista, and Rock Springs, I am forever grateful.

I am certain that conversation was informed by experiences and conversations that went before it, especially those that laid the foundation for naming my belief and expressing the gift of my Christian faith. The faithful ones of Our Lady Immaculate Church; Athol Congregational Church, United Church of Christ (UCC); Joseph Marcotte; Jeffrey and Ann Johnson; and Stacey Eastman Karnowski.

To worship Love is to know Love. To those who taught me love by loving me, and in so doing shaped my experience and understanding of God, I give thanks: my maternal grandfather, Preston Chase; my paternal grandmother, Pia Tarolli; Lorraine and Richard Hennigar; and my first partner in life and ministry, Angel Vernon. Had these threads not been in my life, this book would not have been so woven.

Similarly, if I was not blessed with communities of faith who invited and affirmed my leadership, I would not have had the opportunity to grow with God in designing worship experiences that hold the possibility of God-encounters as liberating and lifegiving as my memorable moment in

Bend. The Federated Church of Bolton, Massachusetts; Chaffin Congregational Church, UCC, Holden, Massachusetts; and Townsend Congregational Church, UCC, Massachusetts, gave me the privilege of leading them in worship when I first entered the ministry. The United Church of Putney, UCC, Vermont; College Street Congregational Church, UCC, Burlington, Vermont; Henniker Congregational Church, UCC, New Hampshire; and Second Congregational Church, UCC, Greenfield, Massachusetts, were open to new expressions of faithfulness, allowed me to be Spirit led in worship planning and leadership, and partnered with me in creating the space for experiencing the Holy in white clapboard, brick-and-mortar, and virtual sanctuaries. To those individuals who assisted in transforming the space with fabric, baskets, flowers, root vegetables, rocks, blocks, pinwheels, balloons, fir garlands, candles, music, storytelling, drama, tableaus, palms, anise stars, quilts, poetry, and pageant masks, on behalf of myself and all who were moved by the colors, sounds, tastes, smells, and touches, I say thank you. Special thanks to the faithful ones in Henniker and Greenfield who read this manuscript and provided me conversation partners about the text, often while living through the ways of experiencing worship described herein. To my sister, Dianne, who blew eggs and balloons, cut paper, colored pictures, sewed whatever I asked for, ran errands, and fed me pasta carbonara when it was all over, thank you. And thanks to my colleagues in the United Church of Christ, especially the Vermont, New Hampshire, and Southern New England Conferences.

After two decades of leading worship, I was led to enter intentional conversation with colleagues, scholars, and saints who might challenge me, equip me, and guide me in defining and articulating my spiritual practice of worship planning and leadership, so that I could share it with others through the writing of this text. I am indebted to the scholars, professors, pastors, and students of Andover Newton Theological Seminary, where I pursued my Doctor of Ministry, including Elizabeth Nordbeck, Robert Pazmino, Burns Stanfield, Thandeka, Christy Lang Hearlson, Benjamin Valentin, Sarah Drummond, and those voices I was introduced to in new ways, including Daniel Goleman, Alexandra Horowitz, Aidan Kavanagh, Thomas Merton, Jaak Panksepp, and Friedrich Schleiermacher.

The effort of sharing the fruit of this beloved and ongoing sacred conversation with you was generously supported by my dear friend Marcia Gagliardi, who has taught me much about writing, publishing,

Gratitude

communicating, and believing in this project. I'm also grateful to the editors and staff of Wipf & Stock Publishers.

But before the professional editors shaped this conversation for public consumption, I was blessed with one who indulged my every thought, my what-ifs, my failures, my late-night craft projects for early-morning rituals, my theological conundrums, my dark nights of the soul, my deep convictions about what is possible, and my dreams of continuing to grow into the fullness of God's intention for me and those I love and serve. She is my worship assistant, my in-house editor, my reader, and my WD-40®, without whom this dream would not have come true. My deepest thanks to Jan, my partner in love, life, and ministry.

Call to Worship

"THANK YOU."

"Good sermon."

"Can we meet next week?"

"Thank you."

"Ugh. I hate that last hymn."

"A little too political, Rev."

"Ran a little over an hour today."

"Have a good week."

It's Sunday morning, and one by one worshippers recess from the sanctuary, greet me at the door, and often feel compelled to offer some evaluative comment on my "performance." As I reflect upon my experience in United Church of Christ congregations, I am uncomfortable with the nature of these comments. While I value the opportunity to look each worshipper in the eye and sincerely greet everyone in the peace of Christ, it's not an ideal context for substantive connection with parishioners and, for some, it quickly becomes a habitual, emotionless ritual at the end of a worship service. I leave my post at the door wondering, "Have you been moved?" "Did you spend the entire time looking at your watch?" "Has this communal sojourn with God, with the Jesus story, and with this gathering of seekers and believers touched your heart, mind, or spirit in a way that leads you into a deeper experience of the Holy?"

A Loss of Connection

There are plenty of statistics and commentaries reflecting the changing landscape of participation in what were once popularly called "mainline Protestant" churches in North America, and the trend is that fewer and fewer friends and neighbors find their spiritual or communal center in the sanctuary of the institutional church. Religious diversity gives us more choices as we seek spiritual community or practices that help us make meaning, situate us in the universe, and restore calm in our lives. Making personal and professional connections no longer revolves around the activities of the church on the green.

And let's be honest: Many mainline Protestant churches have failed to keep pace with effective ways to engage in nurturing a spiritual life, whether through the use of contemporary teaching methods, building civic partnerships for serving the greater good, embracing social media, or designing and redesigning physical space for ministry that is welcoming and sustainable. These factors have diminished the vitality of these faith communities, leading to statistical conclusions about the decline in church attendance and faith in God.

"Were you moved?" "Did this communal sojourn with God, with the Jesus story, and with this gathering of seekers and believers touch your heart, mind, or spirit?"

In the pages that follow, I suggest that the answer to these questions is another crucial component in explaining the decline in church attendance or the rise of the "nones." The loss of sharing an emotional experience of God in the tradition of weekly worship erodes the contemporary relevance of church, as well as the connection between Christian faith and practice in daily life. The messages in the Gospels, the vivid images and parables, are still powerfully relevant to our present lives and future hope; yet, the vibrant stories have become so bogged down in layers of generational interpretation that this vibrancy has been lost to the seekers and believers of the present generation. While we can find moving testimonies and beautiful expressions of the Christian faith throughout the centuries, present-day transformative God-encounters in the context of worship are rare. Worship services have forfeited creating new real-time emotional engagement to cognitive reflection and reasoning upon the experiences of those who have gone before them, poised to talk *about* God rather than experience God.

Repurposing Christian Experience through Generations

In the weaving of church history, different threads of the Christian story have appeared prominent in the tapestry at different times, while others have been set aside. The communal connection to the whole of Jesus' story began to fray almost immediately. From the very beginning of post-resurrection discipleship, reflecting on the arc of Jesus' life and ministry as a generous, instructive, and salvific gesture of God was secondary to a more consuming focus for the regular gathering of the Christ-centered community. The first generation of believers did not anticipate that they were seeding an institution that would endure some two thousand years. They were trying to make sense of the death of their Messiah, experiencing the unique grief of those who knew the earthly Jesus or perhaps knew someone who knew him. Beyond their mourning, they were anticipating Jesus' imminent return, when he would usher in the fullness of God's kingdom. They carried the thread of Jesus' apocalyptic preaching into the first manifestation of "the way." The identity and function of the Jesus movement in the first generation of believers and in each generation to follow were products of a particular cultural context. The defining characteristics of Christian belief and practice in each time and place ever since have resulted in a church with an evolving mission and priorities.

As it became clear that the return of Jesus and the radical transformation followers believed he would bring were not on the immediate horizon, Christian communities began to establish themselves, even if only in secret, as more formal gatherings of belief and practice. Paul and his kindred missionaries picked up the thread of Jesus' moral teaching, distinguishing it from Jewish practice and belief, and let the thread of apocalyptic urgency slip to the background.

In the second through fifth centuries of the Common Era (CE), the primary focus shifted yet again as Christian communities emerged from the secrecy of their house meetings and became more prominent, leading to the official sanctioning of Christianity by Emperor Constantine in the fourth century. Governors and priests were sometimes indistinguishable as the affairs of church and state were comingled for the purpose of civic stability. Constantine's strategy for quelling the simmering unrest of divergent beliefs, before they boiled over, was to commission councils to define the rubric of Christian belief and unity. The primary thread carried in this cultural context was the quest for an intellectual and confessional understanding of the divinity of Jesus and the nature of the triune God.

In time, the doctrinal thread would be split as the "one, holy, catholic, and apostolic" church would formalize different expressions of belief and practice: Roman Catholic, Orthodox, and Protestant, among others. Denominations would follow as communities throughout Christendom wanted to choose the threads that they would work with to weave the fabric of church life, evangelism, and mission, with the main purpose of distinguishing themselves and identifying the members of the group. That diversity in expression was, in part, the fruit of the Enlightenment, which started the ball of individualism and rationalism rolling. In other words, from the very beginning, the Christian church has been more a construct of the values of particular human communities than a continued manifestation of God's activity, calling, and assurance made known in Jesus, even while much good has been done in and through the institution of church.

It seems as though people in Christian communities went from asking "What's next?" to "Who's right and who's wrong?" to "Who's saved and who's not?" to "How do I make this work for me?" In the twentieth century, the church was the place to come together as neighbors, do good works, and build social and economic networks. In the twenty-first century, it's a buyer's market. Sitting alongside those who want to preserve the church they inherited from the generations of family that were founders or pillars in that community are those consumers who are looking for a church that suits their needs, and they'll "church shop" until they find it.

Making the Faith Our Own in Worship

As an ordained pastor in the United Church of Christ in the twenty-first century, I have long embraced the words of invitation and commissioning written in the preamble of the constitution of this denomination, "affirm[ing] the responsibility of the Church in each generation to make this faith its own in reality of worship, in honesty of thought and expression, and in purity of heart before God."[1]

Early in my ministry, I was serving as the pastor of a very small, rural Vermont congregation. The membership had gone through a period of discernment prior to my arrival, deciding to give their communal, institutional existence one more try. When I arrived, there was one family with young children. From the worship leaders who went before me, I inherited an order of worship that included a traditional slot for the "children's message." Each week I would plan a children's message for the possibility that one or both of the young girls would attend worship and perhaps be willing to join me at the front of the sanctuary.

---

1. United Church of Christ, "Preamble to the Constitution."

It didn't take me too long to realize that this was not a viable option. The family had a half-hour commute to church; the father didn't attend regularly; the girls were getting to the age when they opted out as often as their mom would allow; and, if they did attend, they were becoming more self-conscious about being singled out for this public moment in the worship service. Prayerfully, I began to consider the values served by the traditional children's message and wondered if I might tamper with "how it had always been done."

My first decision was to stop requiring that the children come forward. The moment would happen on a weekly basis, as was the custom, but it would be an intergenerational conversation—something along the lines of a "question of the day" that was accessible to all ages. Good things happened, and one good thing led to another, over time. The children were more likely to attend worship and participate because they were not being put on the spot. The adults started to be more engaged within worship and relate to each other more outside of worship. Reflection upon spiritual things became easier and more frequent, not just in worship, but in coffee hour and committee meetings. There was more openness to the idea of God and the activity of the Spirit. We more readily found our story in the Jesus story and vice versa. Sacred aha-moments, energy, caring, and involvement on many levels were on the rise. The deacons began to see themselves more clearly as spiritual leaders. They were equipped, empowered, and sometimes even eager to plan and lead worship. More young families began attending worship and participating in church life, and new relationships blurred the distinctions of age, class, culture, and duration of church membership. Don't be misled. These changes in experience, behavior, and culture did not happen in the first two weeks of worship without a traditional children's message, but there was a gradual evolution that could be traced back to that single change to the worship liturgy.

I believe this was when my intentional commitment to adapting and creating the space for spiritual experience within the context of worship took root. On the whole, the congregation became more flexible in its expectations regarding the morning liturgy. They trusted me, as worship leader, to hold the time and space faithfully and lovingly. Each Advent and Lent season included a progressive ritual that visually evolved over the course of the season. The poetry of contemporary prophets was interspersed with the poetry of the psalmists. Large sheets of solid-colored fabric might be woven as a fire on Pentecost, a river for a baptism, or an unfurling rainbow on Easter morn. Members acted in liturgical dramas, told their stories in sermons and prayers, and led a candlelit carol walk through the village to the sanctuary on Christmas Eve. The conscious act of adapting the worship liturgy for a particular time and place created new life in this small church community and made the gospel and worship living, engaging experiences.

Reclaiming the Emotional Experience of Transformative Worship

One of the gifts of worshipping in the Christian tradition is that we have the opportunity to commingle our stories with the Jesus story and the generations of stories that testify to God's activity in human lives and community. We can keep company with the plaintiff Job. We can have the courage to lay down our nets and follow, or exercise creative problem solving and drop the nets on the other side of the boat. We can stand with the persecuted or the oppressor. We can entertain strangers or be left behind. We can die, and we can rise. In so doing, we identify ourselves in the stories we hear, and our own stories can be revised, repurposed, or resituated in the context of God as Grace, Resurrection, Universal Salvation, or Redemption. My goal in creating transformative worship is to create the space for worshippers to enter into these stories and feel their way into revelation.

I don't want to retell some translation of the Jesus story and simply offer my pedantic interpretation to those gathered. I don't want my agenda as administrator or educator to displace a worshipful invitation to engage the Divine. I want participants to experience the story emotionally in ways that might disturb their equilibrium, contradict their expectations, or use emotional muscles they haven't used in worship for a while, so that they might experience a change of heart or come to recognize God in their midst.

All that we know about the one called God comes from human experience, and human experience rises up from relationship with God, with one another, or with creation. The Bible is not just a tome of wise sayings and morality lessons. The sacred scripture of the Christian tradition is written in the voices of those who have experienced God. In the sanctuary, in the workplace, around the dinner table, on the river, in spiritual practice, in the shadow of loss, or in the trauma of captivity and torture, the experience of God in the land of the living is the activity that shapes belief. From engagement with Divine Mystery to the experience of transformation to the language we use to tell the story, the commentary we have inherited from others is valuable, but the vitality of liturgy comes from bringing ourselves into the space of encounter and testifying to the change we undergo. Moving and meaningful worship happens when those gathered recognize the experience of God in the space of sanctuary or in their daily lives and discover the language to talk about it, using their own words . . . or dance steps, musical rhythms, brushstrokes, hammer and chisel, or street performance.

If we simply rely on the lexicon of belief that has grown out of others' experiences of God, we become increasingly detached from our own God-sightings. We miss out on the opportunity to be compelled, invigorated, comforted, or inspired by our own brush with Divinity.

Attending to Our Focus as Worship Planners

Increasingly, the opportunity to name and reflect upon our religious experiences as a church community mainly happens in worship on Sunday mornings or, less traditionally, a weekday evening worship; that is, the local church community gathers less often throughout the week than it did in prior generations, making Sunday morning the one opportunity for a "captive audience" to welcome and reflect intentionally upon the dance with the Holy. However, as the time church members and friends spend in the church community is reduced to sixty minutes on a Sunday morning, worship and congregation leaders tend to hijack those moments for conducting church business, offering Christian education, and positing ethical mandates under the veil of worship. Too often the focus of the worship planner is to make marketing pitches for one cause or another. Recently, I attended a worship service in which the children's message was a pitch for an exhibit at the local children's museum, the sermon was a passive-aggressive pitch about attending church and trusting that the church will grow, and the service concluded with pitches for the various fundraisers that were being held for church maintenance. I entered the sanctuary longing for a sacred pause, an experience that would reorient me to the gift and strength of my faith, reviving me with the taste of hope and a glimpse of God. Instead, I got one person after another trying to convince me to spend my time or money in a particular way.

The chapters that follow are an invitation to worship planners in Protestant Christian churches (particularly in a North American context) to attend to the design and substance of weekly worship services, with the goal of creating the space for deeply felt God-encounters within the context of the worship experience. You will be encouraged to peel back the layers that have increasingly diminished the worship experience, making it an opportunity to talk *about* theology, ethics, or local church business, and reimagine the time of worship as an active engagement of the senses, as well as the mind, holding the potential for aha-moments that are felt, often before they are understood. You will be given the permission, encouragement, and tools to strengthen your spiritual practice of *attentiveness*, especially as it relates to planning and leading worship in ways that effectively transform individual lives, as well as the life and ministry of the local church.

With illustrations from my practice of ministry, and prompts for reader reflection and engagement, this is a beckoning for worship leaders to embrace a regular practice of intentional, fluid discernment, informing the expression of their Christian experience and belief in worship planning, which can be used to create liturgies that hold the possibility of transforming local churches—their members, their relationships, their relevance, and their reach.

1

Attending to Worship as an Emotional Experience

> *Paying Attention to Spiritual Experience*
>
> Bring into your heart and mind the memory of a transformative spiritual experience or God-encounter. It could be the first time you believed in God or an experience when you were somehow convinced there is a God.
>
> When did you experience a brush with the Divine?
>
> Where were you? Bring the location back to life in your mind.
>
> Who was with you?
>
> How were you feeling *before* you noticed the Holy in your midst?
>
> What happened, causing you to be moved or changed?
>
> How did you feel in that moment?

IT IS SAFE TO say that most transformative spiritual experiences are emotional experiences. When asked to recount a memorable encounter with the one they call Creator, Redeemer, Sustainer, or God by another name, most people will talk about how they *felt* in that moment. Observe Jesus or those who were healed by him, the medieval mystics, an evangelical

Christian megachurch, or a pilgrim at the Wailing Wall, and it is obvious that spiritual experiences are very often emotional experiences. They are felt experiences, which only later, in a matter of moments or over a period of time, are reflected upon and understood enough to be named.

On my best days as a worship planner and leader, it has been my goal to create the space for worshippers to enter into that sacred place of a God-encounter, whether in joy, gratitude, thirst, despair, or wonder. Pastor and musician Burns Stanfield says, "Worship is the practice of our faith and hope—it is a practice session."[1] In that spirit, I plan worship as if it were an invitation for the worshippers to experience their faith in God by being *moved* to a feeling of hope, however that may be defined in the moment. No matter what else is going on in the life of the congregation, in the world outside the walls of the sanctuary, in the relationships that I hold with individual worshippers, *I enter the moment of worship with the intention of providing an opportunity for those gathered to have a transformative spiritual experience.* I want worshippers to go out into the world as practiced believers, having felt something and knowing such God-encounters are possible and may shape their lives in the congregation, in personal relationships, and in the world beyond the sanctuary.

Getting Distracted

That is my goal in worship planning on my best days, but I must confess that I have not always had my best days when planning worship. I have fallen into the same traps that have ensnared others. Recently, I had the opportunity to observe the ways we can get distracted or worship can get hijacked as I worshipped with a number of different United Church of Christ congregations. Rarely did I leave those worship services feeling as if I had even flirted with a transformative spiritual experience. I have often wondered what it was that the worship leaders attended to as they planned worship. The focus often seems to be on the sermon, with the surrounding liturgy never straying from the tried-and-true checklist of the expected. The sermon may be an attempt at educating the listener about scripture or God, it may strive to make a point about something in the church's life that everyone "needs to hear," or it may fall in step with the theme of the day as published in the denominational calendar. In the end, it seems the worship leaders want the worshippers to leave the sanctuary having *learned*

1. Stanfield, "Liturgical Calendar."

Attending to Worship as an Emotional Experience

something—having informed their minds rather than having experienced a change of heart. Let me provide some examples of what I experienced when sitting in the pews as a worship attendee.

Educating and Advocating

One of the services I experienced was a quintessential illustration of the Protestant Reformation that it celebrated that day. As worship began, there was an extensive explanation of the Protestant Reformation. Later in the service, there was "A Special Moment," during which the pastor shared an anecdote and encouraged people to vote in the upcoming election. There was, in lieu of a sung anthem, some readings from Martin Luther's thoughts *about* hymn singing. The sermon, an intellectual reflection on Zacchaeus (including a not-so-veiled, derogatory reference to a presidential nominee), included an excerpt from an article by political commentator David Brooks. The service ended without any sort of invitation to connect with the Mystery that fueled the Reformation and that beckons us into relationship with the Still-Speaking God.

The entire service was an experience for the mind, a cognitive exercise. It was a service in which someone may have learned a thing or two, but I do not believe anyone left having *felt* anything that could count as an encounter with God. I was reminded of how Word-centered the Reformed worship service is, which has led to the centrality of the sermon and its lesson. This focus on learning leads church folk to say they want to leave worship with "something to *think* about." However, when worship becomes only an intellectual exercise, it loses its reason for being; it loses the opportunity to be an act of faith and to draw worshippers into an emotional experience of God and community.

Harboring Ulterior Motives

In another service, there was a big annual meeting of the congregation on the horizon. It was budget time. There were difficult staffing decisions to be made. There was the question of "to sell or not to sell" the nineteenth-century house that had served as the parsonage for all 150 years of the church's existence. The antiquated organizational structure required more people to fill the slots on committees than the number of actively engaged members, so there was a 40-percent shortfall of volunteers at any given time, and there were vulnerable people and places beyond the church community needing the hands and feet of Christ in the world. The worship service was book-ended with a litany of announcements regarding the administrative business of the church. The sermon was a defense for full-time pastoral ministry. The prayers were not relevant to the context of life within or beyond the church community, and the whole service was abbreviated because the leadership was planning to meet after worship to plan the annual meeting and wanted to get started as soon as possible.

Any hope of creating the space for a felt experience of the Holy was hijacked by the agendas of church leaders. I couldn't help but wonder how much more successful the members' engagement in the annual meeting and the ministry of the congregation might be if careful worship planning in the weeks before the meeting included preparing hearts and minds for faithful discipleship and discernment by inviting emotional connections with God and each other.

Misappropriating Ministry with Children

During another service that I attended, it was the "Children's Moment" that was a blatant departure from building an emotional, spiritually enlivening experience. The children were invited forward to circle around the pastor. The pastor read seven or eight wise sayings from one of those books that is filled with children's wisdom (similar to *Children's Letters to God*). She then read three or four proverbs from what she called "the funny little book in the Bible called Proverbs." In the midst of reading one proverb, she said to the blank-faced children, "This one is really for the adults; you probably won't understand it." Then the children were dismissed to class. She never asked them a question. She consistently used language and references that were likely unintelligible to many of the children. She never elicited an emotional response or made a personal connection.

Too often children are made to feel like props in "The Moment with Children" or the annual children's Christmas pageant. Many times, pastors offer a children's message that is really just a more entertaining version of the adult sermon, hoping that the adults will get the message in one moment or the other. As a result, the children are confused and the adults become spectators, neither of which contributes to a positive, visceral moment of transformation for children or adults.

Attending to Worship as an Emotional Experience

> *Paying Attention to Pitfalls in Worship Planning and Leadership*
>
> Review liturgies and sermons from recent worship services you have planned and led.
> Based upon the structure and content of the service, what would you say you were paying attention to as you planned each service?
> What do you wish you could have paid more attention to?
> What distractions derailed your effort?

Adjusting the Focus of Worship Planning and Leadership

If worship in mainline Protestant churches is going to be relevant in Western contemporary culture, it needs to be in the business of engaging hearts as well as heads. If Christian faithfulness is going to be a factor in the experience of daily life, it needs to be felt in the gut, not just understood in the mind. While Daniel Goleman, author of *Focus: The Hidden Driver of Excellence*, does not write about church, he does write about the stewardship of attention. He asserts, "Directing attention toward where it needs to go is a primal task of leadership."[2] It is incumbent upon worship leaders to prayerfully design a worship service that leads to a change of heart, a transformative spiritual experience or God-encounter that shapes belief. That, in turn, may equip the worshipper with a visceral orientation toward Christian faithfulness—hope, compassion, peace with justice—in a society where what is good and right as well as truthful is increasingly difficult to define.

You may note that I am speaking about "worship planning and leadership," not "sermon preparation." Seminary preaching courses often tell students that they must have a "purpose" for their sermons. Early in my career, I admit I followed this advice, and it became part of my toolbox. It was helpful to pray my way into identifying the purpose for my sermon; I often wrote that purpose in the form of a prayer at the top of my sermon draft, referring to it frequently for guidance. However, I have now expanded that practice so that this prayer and purpose guide the entire service. If, to borrow from Goleman, the leader is charged with directing the attention of the

---

2. Goleman, *Focus*, 209.

worshipper toward where it needs to go, then the worship planner ought to have a purpose for the entirety of the worship service, not just the sermon.

For example, on Homecoming Sunday we may hear the words of the psalmist who offered us Psalm 139:

> Where can I go from your spirit?
> Or where can I flee from your presence?
> If I ascend to heaven, you are there;
> if I make my bed in Sheol, you are there.
> If I take the wings of the morning
> and settle at the farthest limits of the sea,
> even there your hand shall lead me,
> and your right hand shall hold me fast.
> If I say, "Surely the darkness shall cover me,
> and the light around me become night,"
> even the darkness is not dark to you;
> the night is as bright as the day,
> for darkness is as light to you.[3]

The entire worship experience—prayers, reflection, conversation, physical space, ritual, and music—should be shaped around what it looks and feels like to be welcomed home, whether returning to church after the summer scatter and joyfully reuniting with friends, finding church when life is especially difficult and there is no place that feels like home, or sitting in the pew you've sat in for decades and holding a new, traumatic truth in the privacy of your being. This should not just be a day when we get back into the routine of church and register the children for Sunday school. I want the worshippers to feel the gift and responsibility of church being the home where those who cross the threshold know that there is no place they can go to elude the promise and presence of God.

As worship planner and leader, I attempt to cultivate the entire space of worship, as well as the space in the hearts and minds of worshippers, to make room for divine aha-moments. My goal is to loosen the cognitive reins and welcome the freedom of intimate, emotional experience, which just may lead to transformative encounters with the Spirit. It is in that moment, which some may call the "thin place" of communing with God, where the worshipper is moved, belief is ignited, and testimony is written on the heart. Here's what attending to worship as an emotional experience looked like at the opening of a worship service I planned and led on Easter morning.

---

3. Ps 139:1–7, NRSV. All biblical references are to this version of the Bible.

Worship as Emotional Experience: An Illustration

The storytelling had begun in a worship service on Palm Sunday and continued through the Maundy Thursday Tenebrae, both foreshadowing the darkness of Good Friday since there was no formal service on that day. While the worshippers had been mildly surprised and intrigued by the palms that lined the walkway into the church and up the center aisle of the sanctuary on Palm Sunday, many were completely disoriented when they walked into the church on Easter morning.

The striking Palm Sunday arrangement of pussy willows and palms still graced the altar as it had the week before, and there was nary an Easter lily in sight. The traditional list of Easter flower donations was in the bulletin, but the only adornments in the chancel area were black cloths. Couples were whispering and wondering, "Where are the flowers?" "Where are the candles?" The Communion table was draped in black, the remnants of the previous days scattered upon it: a clay plate and a tipped cup, a crown of thorns, and a few palms. The musical prelude was not a grand, lively celebration of resurrection, but a mournful pastorale played by a string quartet. We hadn't arrived at the empty tomb just yet.

The service began, not with the usual warm welcome to worship, but with a dramatic setting of the scene with an excerpt from "The Day Peter Ran," an interpretation of John 20:1–9 by Ralph F. Wilson:

> By day it gnawed at him, but nights were even worse. He had betrayed his dearest friend. Not privately, not secretly, but blatantly, out in the open for all the world to see. And now it was too late to say, "I'm sorry." His friend was dead.
>
> Peter tossed sleeplessly, unable to find a position that felt comfortable. Outside he could hear the sounds of Jerusalem stirring to life. This city he had once loved to visit, he now hated. It held too many painful memories impossible to erase from his mind. Today he would leave for Galilee and fishing, though even fishing held no allure for him now. Nothing did.[4]

---

4. Wilson, "Day Peter Ran."

When the reader sat down, the choir began the haunting song "If I Had Been," asking questions of the listeners.

> If I had been in Jerusalem on that day . . .
> would I have left my Savior's side or would I stay?
> . . . if I had spent all that time with him,
> if I had been his trusted friend, what could have torn me away?
> If I had witnessed his miracles and believed,
> would I have stayed by my Savior's side or would I leave?
> If I had seen all that he could do,
> if I had known what he would go through,
> if I were one of his chosen few, what could have torn me away?
> He healed the eyes that were blind from birth;
> he made them see somehow . . .
> why can't they see the truth now?
> If I had been in Jerusalem . . .
> would I be willing to give my life for him, as he did for me?[5]

The reading of Peter's story continued until he and John were left wondering, "What if . . . What if he is risen?" Only then did the choir herald the news with an introit, first sung in unison, then as a round.

> Christ is arisen!
> Alleluia! Alleluia! Alleluia! Alleluia!
> Christ is arisen! Christ is arisen![6]

After creating this portal through which those present could enter into the story, we finally named what was happening as we were called to worship:

> Leader: When we are all despairing;
> When the world is full of grief;
> When we see no way ahead,
> And hope has gone away:
> All: Roll back the stone.
> Although we fear change;
> Although we are not ready;
> Although we'd rather weep and run away:
> Roll back the stone.

---

5. Schram, *If I Had Been*.
6. Traditional, composer/lyricist unknown.

Attending to Worship as an Emotional Experience

> Leader: Because we're coming with the women;
> Because we hope where hope is vain;
> Because you call us from the grave and show the way:
> All: Roll back the stone.[7]

As congregants then raised their voices in praise with "Christ the Lord is risen today," the sanctuary was transformed *before their eyes* into a tableau of Easter joy. Black cloths were removed. Pots of colorful Easter lilies, tulips, and daffodils were carried up the center aisle and tucked into the reedy pussy willows and drying palms. More flowers were placed around the altar, the chancel, and the Communion table. The color of life was abundant. The Communion table was cleared of the symbols of a meal shared in sadness and set with the symbols of a meal to be shared in hope. As the rousing chorus came to an end, the candles were lit and the gathered community centered itself in prayer:

> In the beginning was the Word, and the Word was with God, and the Word was God. He was in the beginning with God. All things came into being through him, and without him not one thing came into being. What has come into being in him was life, and the life was the light of all people. The light shines in the darkness, and the darkness did not overcome it. (John 1:1–5)

> When we are thankful for the gift of life, a place to call home, and the freedom to make our own choices, we call you Gratitude, O God.
> When we get a great idea, plant a new garden, or exercise our imagination, we call you Creativity, O God.
> When we mend a broken relationship, are released from a debt, or are given a second chance, we call you Forgiveness, O God.
> When we feel calm in our solitude, find comfort with a pet, experience a trust in the truth that all will be well, we call you Peace, O God.

---

7. Morley, *Bread of Tomorrow*, 122.

This Time with Feeling

> When we celebrate a newborn, see the stories in the faces of our elders, or drink in the view of a majestic mountain, we call you Beauty, O God.
>
> When sobriety trumps addiction, clarity cuts through confusion, and new information helps us cope with chronic illness, we call you Light, O God, and today we rejoice that darkness has not overcome it.[8]

Creating Primary Theologians

Those who met Jesus in his earthly life, or gathered together in the wake of his death, did not follow a rubric for Christian worship when they met to explore or express their pilgrimage in faith and orient themselves to God in thanks and praise. They may have borrowed from the traditions they knew and sung the Psalms, made music with homemade instruments, shared an offering, prayed for one another, or recounted the stories of how God or Jesus changed their lives, but there were no Orders of Christian Worship bequeathed to them as first-century church. First-hand testimony of God- or Jesus-encounters rippled through and beyond the circles of the faithful. Two thousand years later, worshippers gathering in mainline Protestant sanctuaries can experience that same energy of sharing similar first-hand encounters with their God.

In many worship services today, we are attempting to lead people into Christian belief and practice by using "secondary theology," written primarily by early church "fathers." Instead, as worship planners and leaders, we ought to turn our attention to the character of the very events that authored much of the liturgy and doctrine that we rely upon in our Christian tradition—the power of transformative spiritual experiences that compel us to testify in word and deed.

Roman Catholic priest and liturgical theologian Aidan Kavanagh identifies the transformative spiritual experience that might occur in the event of worship as a change of heart. It is the necessary prerequisite to what he calls "primary theology."[9] Worshippers become theologians in that moment when, consciously or subconsciously, they experience a change of heart. The instant we think about, talk about, or write about the change

---

8. Tarolli, worship service, First Church in Jaffrey, NH, April 5, 2015.
9. Kavanagh, *On Liturgical Theology*, 74.

of heart we experienced, we are engaging in "secondary theology," one or more steps removed from the activity of God that reverberated in a person or community. We do not *think* our way into a life in the Spirit. We may willfully position ourselves for a sojourn with the Sacred, but the aha-moment, the awesome bliss, the rescue from out of nowhere, and the gift of faith itself are spontaneous surprises of Holy Generosity, washing over us as Divine Awareness.

The use of the term divine awareness rather than the oft-prayed-for divine intervention is intentional. When we are poised for God-encounters, we are not waiting on God to engage us; rather, we are orienting ourselves so that we might experience the ever-present God. One hazard of the traditional anthropomorphic or metaphorical language Christians use for describing a God that is larger than our human vocabulary and our wildest imagination is that we then tend to objectify God rather than experience God. We pray for Divine Intervention rather than recognizing the revelation of an abiding Divine Presence. We ask for God's blessing rather than standing in the light of having already been blessed. We confuse righteousness with impressive knowledge or good deeds that please rather than something much more visceral. If piety is reduced to *knowing* or *doing*, then pastoral ministry becomes an act of education, convincing, or program planning. Engaging the emotional human experience, where our stories are written and animated, becomes a happy accident at best.

Offering an alternative to the more traditional "God as entity" thinking, in his seminal work *The Christian Faith*, theologian Friedrich Schleiermacher equates God with a particular state of human consciousness.[10] Affirming that all religious experience is human experience, the image of God will always bear a human imprint. However, instead of *making* God in our image, Schleiermacher suggests that we *meet* God in our experience. Piety is the shift in feeling or change of heart that allows us to momentarily suspend ourselves in a space of absolute dependence that Schleiermacher calls "God-consciousness." What makes Jesus distinct in his divinity, according to Schleiermacher, is the fact that he was never disconnected from that feeling of God-consciousness. The rest of us are fortunate to glimpse it on occasion. Focusing our attention on creating the space for such a possibility in the context of worship will transform individual and communal lives.

---

10. The ideas in this paragraph are gleaned from Schleiermacher, *Christian Faith*, v–31.

This Time with Feeling

Returning to the liturgy I created for the festival worship on Easter morning, perhaps there are some who would not even contemplate disrupting the annual traditions of a particular congregation in such a dramatic way. I understand the fear worship leaders may feel around creating new liturgies and altering inherited worship traditions. So, I would just like to share with you some of the comments I heard in the days following that Easter service.

"Something happened
in church today!"

"There was curiosity because
it was different
from the moment
we walked in the door."

"It was the most moving
Easter worship experience
I have ever had."

A mother said her 5-year-old daughter asked,
"Where's Jesus?" as she sat on the edge of her pew,
listening to the story unfold.

"It was the first time
I felt like I really experienced
Easter."

"When I saw my young granddaughter days later,
she was still asking questions.
When she asked 'Why were the black cloths there?'
it gave us the opportunity
to share more of the story with her."

As I pointed out at the beginning of the call to worship, post-worship comments are not typically very revealing of what actually occurred for people relative to their inner experience during worship, but there was something different about these comments. There was a palpable shift in the energy of the individuals and the community. The "something" that "happened" wasn't just about the drama; it was about the emotional shifts that unfolded as a result of the drama. I say "Thanks be to God" for the color, sound, word, silence, story, community, planning, invitation, space, language, and movement that create such an experience, and for the Net of Grace that holds it all. Now, let's explore how to make that "something" also "happen."

2

Attending to the Language of Worship: Words

BEFORE WORDS, THERE WERE pictures. Before pictures, messages were conveyed by vocal tone or bodily gesture. Humans have been communicating since the beginning of time, and each innovation in communication, from cave to conference table, from desert altar to cathedral, has been a product of human construction. Language—drawn on rocks, expressed on faces, sculpted with bodies, harmonized in a concert hall, spoken in a thoughtful whisper, tweeted in emojis, or bellowed from a soapbox—is a system of communication, but the particular system chosen by humans in the Judeo-Christian era and used to shape the way we talk about God has primarily consisted of words.[1]

Words create a context for talking about the ineffable, the Holy Mystery that has been called God by generations of believers, seekers, agnostics, and atheists alike. From the beginning, our understanding of God has been shaped by a language that is limited to the vocabulary, context, and experience of the human believers. The essence and activity of God are only glimpsed in the images illustrated by our verbal language, as the context and experience from which we reap our words are but fleeting wisps of all that comes from or points to the Holy One of Blessing.

The words chosen for storytelling, teaching, and worship represent the leanings of a particular individual or community in a specific time and

---

1. Karen Armstrong is a British author and a member of the Jesus Seminar who has done extensive writing on the history of religions, especially Christianity. In *A History of God*, she offers an excellent overview of the evolution of religious belief and language, effectively illustrating the ways in which language shaped religious expression and thought in the earliest stages of the monotheistic faith traditions.

place. The prevailing language that came to define the Christian tradition was shaped by the words and images of biblical times, a strand of polytheism, a strand of Greek philosophy, and a strand of emerging monotheism.[2] While forever incomplete, because a language of human construction cannot possibly encompass the fullest depth and breadth of the Divine One, the words and images that were used then would shape the Christian tradition for at least two millennia. Now, in the twenty-first century, that linguistic heritage is both lush and limited.

The Blessing and Limitation of Age-Old Refrains

There are countless instances when committed or casual Christians, faced with significant trial or trauma, instinctively recite the Lord's Prayer or the Twenty-Third Psalm or sing "Amazing Grace," "We Shall Overcome," or "Rock of Ages." Held hostage by armed guards, gripped by overwhelming grief, surprised by the harrowing circumstances of natural disasters, survivors have reflexively found comfort in those prayers, scripture passages, and songs of their faith that were imprinted on their hearts long ago, words that have been passed from generation to generation, capturing a promise that abides in all situations, all times, and all places.

Developing a broader linguistic expression of belief and practice does not mean dismissing out of hand the words that have sustained the saints who have gone before us and that are still cherished by many today. Instead, expanding the lexicon of our worship liturgies invites the possibility of composing new refrains that may echo through prisons, fields of debris, hospital emergency rooms, and wounded hearts in present and future generations.

When I was serving a church in Vermont, which shares the moniker of "least religious state in the union" with its neighbor New Hampshire, I learned that the Lord's Prayer was not always included in the weekly worship service because the people who gathered on Sunday morning weren't comfortable with the language of any one version. It was then that a new aspect of my pastoral practice took root. Because I value the prayer as one

---

2. Love, war, wine, the sea, the harvest, and the hearth were all assigned their own god in the land of many gods, and the created world was simply subject to their whim. In the same marketplace, there would be those who spoke the language of Greek philosophy and, if they were so inclined to cautiously believe in the God of monotheism, it was the transcendence of God that they emphasized: belief in the eternity of God, the necessity of God, and the immutability of God. This other-worldly understanding resulted in the same distancing from God as was evident in the polytheistic culture.

that binds generations of disciples to Jesus and to one another in all times and places, and because I often imagine a chorus of the prayer resonating around the globe at any given time, I like to include it in weekly worship. However, I didn't want language to be an obstacle to participation. My hope was that those in this circle of worship could feel comfortable lending their voices to the prayer with intention—hearing or speaking testimony, finding inspiration or perspective, or centering themselves in the Holy—and nurture community through the sharing of communal prayer. So, I simply invited folks to join in echoing the prayer that Jesus taught us, *using their own words*. I encouraged them to add their voices to the chorus of the faithful and be comforted by the familiar cadence of a common prayer and a tie that binds, even if one said "trespasses" and another said "sins," one said "kingdom" and another said "kin-dom," or one said "Father" and another said "Mother," "Creator," "Lover," or "Redeemer." Perhaps others would slip in and out of two different languages. I invited them to gently hold a tradition, carefully passing it to the next generation of believers, but allowing and affirming each unique voice so that the ritual could be meaningful and hold the possibility of a God-encounter.

Many of us have had the experience of wearing clothing that doesn't fit quite right. As we wear it, all we can do is think about the places it pinches or sags, hoping others won't notice.

A flexible regard for well-worn prayers and hymns encourages the task of spiritual reflection, discerning an expression for a better fit, so that the worshipper is not distracted by words that chafe, but can relax into nurturing a substantive connection with God. That being said, sometimes no matter what you do to your threadbare jeans or your beloved college sweatshirt, they're still not going to fit as well as they once did. Nonetheless, you hang on to them, even patch them and mend them, for sentimental purposes.

> *Paying Attention to Age-Old Refrains*
>
> Choose one of your favorite prayers, psalms, or hymns that you turn to for inspiration, anchoring, or reassurance. Speak it or sing it aloud in a spirit of prayer. Take a moment to be grateful for the gift of these words.
>
> What is it about this refrain that has made it one of your favorites?

Rewrite the prayer, passage, or hymn, using words and images from the context of your daily life. How might this contemporary version of an age-old refrain be used in the context of a worship service, creating the space for recognizing anew the Holy in the familiar? (See Appendix 1 for an illustration of reimagining the age-old refrain of Psalm 23.)

Guiding the Congregation's Attention to the Lord's Prayer

I have used a version of the following exercise successfully as the basis of a weekly Lenten prayer gathering as well as a conversational summer sermon series. While the exercise gives participants permission to edit particular words in the prayer, keeping the same general content and cadence, another invitation is to write a whole new version of the prayer. The former equips worshippers to still pray the Lord's Prayer in community, even if a word changes here or there; the latter can be used, on occasion, in place of the traditional Lord's Prayer during communal worship. Both are affirmations of praying in our own words:

Slowly speak aloud the version of the Lord's Prayer that comes easiest to you. Repeat it a few times, relaxing into the emotional rhythms of the prayer.

What do you feel as you say the prayer?

Slowly repeat the prayer a few more times, being mindful of the words.

Imagine having a dialogue with Jesus, the teacher of the prayer, about words or phrases that give you pause. Paraphrase the meaning of the prayer in your own words.

Slowly repeat the prayer, allowing yourself to use words that resonate with how you experience the prayer as testimony, inspiration, or assurance.

Attending to the Language of Worship: Words

The Blessing and Limitation of Biblical Images

> *Paying Attention to Your Vision of God*
>
> This exercise can be done with a pencil on paper, paint on canvas, molding clay in your hands, or drawing with your finger in the sand. Sophistication of expression is not important. Stick figures and symbols work fine. Draw, paint, or sculpt how you understand or experience God in relation to yourself. Without revising your artistic expression, describe what you have created and why. Tell the story of your image of God.

Often when I'm sitting with those who have come to me for support in their spiritual journeys, I listen closely to their words to get a sense of where they understand God to be in the midst of their lives, dilemmas, or desires. If talking about God doesn't come naturally to them without my prompting, then I will invite them to do this drawing exercise. When they are finished drawing, I ask them to describe what they have created.

More times than not, God is an entity separate from the person. God has been the water pouring out of a watering can onto a flower that represents the individual. God has been a point in the universe, distant from the individual standing on earth. And, even with adults, God has sometimes been a bearded grandfather figure. It is a wonderful starting place for conversation as I first learn about the images they use to define their experience. Then I discover what the image conveys about people's understanding of their relationship with God, be it how they understand their identity as children of God or their interpretation of where God is in the midst of their here and now. Often, I find that we are then unpacking their "embedded theology." That is, we are discovering how their understanding and experience of God was shaped in childhood or at some other pivotal time in their lives. Frequently, it is an understanding that has not kept pace with their emotional and intellectual development. In addition, the phrases and stories they once learned no longer offer them the building blocks of a belief they can now embrace. For the same reason Jesus taught with parables, we then begin to explore language, imagery, and belief that grows out of and speaks to them in their daily lives.[3]

People who live on farms and raise their own food are often warned not to name the animals that will one day land in their freezer because it will make the anticipated slaughter that much more difficult. When we name pets or things, we give them a new dimension, at least in our hearts and minds. As soon as we give something—our pets, plants, or cars—a name, we deepen our relationship with it and, as humans, we begin to project our language and our way of being onto these non-human entities. Our cats become our children and our conversation partners. Our plants turn their faces toward the heavens and sing the praises of God. Our cars get pleaded with, yelled at, caressed, or kicked based upon their performance, as if these inanimate objects could choose to behave differently.

In the same way, ever since human beings have experienced higher powers in their lives, they have named them, spoken to them and about them, using the only words they have, the vernacular of their particular time and place as well as the vocabulary bequeathed to them. Thus begins the making of myths, stories of human encounters with the Divine.[4] God creates, leads, talks, holds, chastises, weeps, dreams, punishes, gives and takes away life. God is Living Water and Blowing Wind. God is the King of Kings, Lord of Lords, Everlasting Father, and Prince of Peace.

Jesus had his own practice of translation. To his audience in an agrarian society with an oppressive ruling class, he spoke about mustard seeds, fig trees, sheep and goats, and a woman at a well. He told stories about tax collectors, Pharisees, judges, wealthy ones, and royalty. While the truths he sought to teach were, at times, the very same ones from his Jewish background, he interpreted them in a language that would be meaningful to his contemporaries.

The images that are more personal, identifying God as an active participant in the universe, particularly in the human community, contribute

---

3. In his book *Thinking Through Our Faith*, C. David Grant orients the reader to the questions of theological interpretation and appropriation in the twenty-first century. He encourages thinkers and practitioners of faith to articulate a theology that respects and integrates contemporary thought, understanding, and experience in various cultural disciplines, i.e., science, history, sociology, and nature.

4. Theologian Paul Tillich points out in *Dynamics of Faith* that "Myths are always present in every act of faith because the language of faith is the symbol . . . It puts the stories of the gods into the framework of time and space although it belongs to the nature of the ultimate to be beyond time and space" (56).

to the building of relationships among humanity, creation, and "the Father, Son, and Holy Spirit." We can identify the source and sustenance of our lives in God as Parent or Partner, and we can be cared for and guided by God as Shepherd. We can be rewarded by our King. We can walk the way of life, defend ourselves, and be given our daily bread by a personified God. There are countless images of God in the pages of Christian scripture. The Bible is, after all, a chronicle of God-encounters told in the language of a culture that experienced life through the family unit, in an agrarian society, with a ruling class, i.e., Father, Shepherd, King. It was in a specific context that the authors of Genesis and Job and John recorded their glimpses of the Sacred and their understanding of God's activity in the world. But those images do not always speak easily to contemporary listeners, who wouldn't know a fig tree if they were sitting in one and have never even seen a well, much less drawn water from one with a bucket; they don't pay bills with talents, and they don't store their Chianti in wineskins.

Through the centuries, within different cultures, scholars have skillfully translated Aramaic, Hebrew, Greek, and Latin into familiar and contemporary words in an effort to convey those inspired testimonies to the generations that followed. Expanding the language of our Christian faith affords modern-day spiritual pilgrims an opportunity to discover or create a lexicon of faith that incorporates their own experience, knowledge, and vernacular, reclaiming or reframing a meaningful relationship with God, Jesus, and Spirit.

One of the most reliable metaphors for my image and experience of God is the ocean. If God were a science to be defined and proven, the properties of God and the properties of the ocean would share many parallels, I believe. The ocean is vast. Mystery lies beyond the horizon. There is no beginning or ending. It can be powerful and placid. In its persistent movement, it can transform solids. It holds and sustains life, and it has a rhythm. The ebb and flow of the tides are reminders to me of the comings and goings, the ups and downs, the beginnings and endings, the necessary flip sides of life. The tides may change in their particularities, but the constancy of presence and movement is as close to being visibly eternal as I can witness in my earthly life. Living and worshipping in New England, not too far from the shores of the Atlantic Ocean, this image makes it into my prayers and illustrations on a regular basis.

The use of metaphors releases us into a whole new pool of expressions for approaching our belief and practice.[5] Identifying metaphors from the context and daily life of the community in which you lead worship is one way of making the vocabulary of belief and practice more accessible to those who find biblical imagery to be archaic or irrelevant. In addition, worship leaders may use those contemporary images or experiences to usher the worshippers into an emotional response that creates the space for God-encounters or aha-moments. God as the gardener tending a vegetable garden, God as the light streaming through the woods, God as GPS or smartphone, God as railway or freeway, God as life growing up through the ashes; these are all images that can be developed to create an invitation into spiritual experience and expression.

Paying Attention to Metaphorical Images

Make a list of images or experiences that are constant or meaningful for you in your daily life. Choose one of the images or experiences you have listed and reflect upon God, faith, or discipleship using that image or experience. For example:

God is like the wind because . . .
Faith is like a cactus because . . .
Discipleship is like a video game because . . .

Spend several minutes attending to that one image or experience, completing the sentence with various words and phrases. Consider using the imagery you have discovered in prayers or illustrations during a worship service or Bible study.

Guiding the Congregation's Attention to Metaphorical Images

Consider using the following exercise with the group in your church that is responsible for worship planning and leadership.

---

5. For an introduction to how metaphors can provide different lenses for seeing things in a new way, see Andy Eklund's article "How to Use Metaphors to Inspire Creative Thinking," at http://www.andyeklund.com/metaphors-and-creative-thinking/.

Attending to the Language of Worship: Words

It is an engaging conversation to open a regular meeting or a fun way to nurture spiritual reflection and build relationships during a retreat. Typically, I ask participants to reflect in silence for a period of time, jotting down words or pictures that come to mind, and then invite them to share with one another.

1. Which biblical images for God (faith or practice) do you resonate with the most and why?

2. Are there particular biblical images that are relied upon more often than others in the context of your worship service? Conversely, are there images that you avoid? Be honest.

3. Make a list of images or experiences that are constant or meaningful for you in your daily life.

4. Choose one of the images or experiences you have listed and reflect upon God (faith or discipleship) using that image or experience. God is like _____ because _____.

5. Spend several minutes attending to that one image or experience, completing the sentence with various words and phrases.

Consider how you might use these images in the context of worship, with the hope that those gathered may also discover them as snapshots of the Holy in their midst.

The Blessing and Limitation of Theological Terms

The sandbox hosting serious, thoughtful play with the language of the Christian faith has primarily been contained within the academy. Wise and faithful scholars explore new ways to understand and express God's holy intention—past, present, and future—and their diligent, creative work provides stimulating fodder in seminary classrooms and at religious conferences worldwide. It can be inspiring to wallow in God-talk with those who seek to unveil the life-giving possibilities of beloved sacred texts and the enduring covenant shared between the Creator and created.

But these conversations happen to a much lesser degree among the people in the pews and pulpits of local churches. Instead, in the worship and work of the congregation, laypersons and clergy alike play "hot potato" with the words they have inherited from generations past. The words "sin," "salvation," "redemption," and "confession" identify important aspects of living the fullness of a Christian life, but they spit and sizzle as they sit on the coals of layers of interpretation and use. They may be comfort to some and alien to others. Some believers have adopted a viable formulaic definition for each. Others who *want* to believe have an increasing number of holes in the fabric of their language and liturgy as they choose not to use words they cannot grasp or accept. As a result, many twenty-first-century believers and seekers lose interest in the pursuit of their spiritual journeys, unable to find enough workable threads to weave together a personal or communal faith.

I am reminded of my impish childhood practice of lying in bed and picking at the layers of wallpaper on my bedroom wall. It was a room with at least four generations of style. After I left it some thirty-five years ago, it gained yet one more layer of wallpaper, but that would be the last of my family's contributions. It is often the case that the interior designs of homes and the styles of wardrobes eventually reach their stasis. Perhaps at some point the thought of further change overwhelms the desire to stay current with style. Or maybe the evolution of styles and modern conveniences outpaces one's perceived needs. Stasis can be a goal, but it is more often a familiar convenience or a consequence of neglect. Stasis is achieved and maintained in churches, too. The carpets, artwork, upholstery, office furniture, and pew cushions often testify to it, and so does the language of our work and worship.

Over time, biblical and traditional language evolved from being stories of the sacred to being tagged as the sacred itself. Newcomers to the faith were told what to believe rather than encouraged to tell their own stories of their human-Divine encounters, as their spiritual ancestors had recorded in scripture. Devotion to both the personal and impersonal metaphors has anchored the Christian tradition in essentially the same place, linguistically if not theologically, with *relatively* little movement since the fourth century CE.

The distance in time and space that has accumulated since then is vast, and the consequences of not keeping pace with the tides of time, experience, and knowledge are severe. Not only have the metaphors become

Attending to the Language of Worship: Words

anachronistic, but there is an assumed sacredness around the metaphors that grew out of a particular time and place, and a presumption that one size should fit all no matter how many centuries have passed. The experiential distance between the first believers and those of the twenty-first century is enormous, and yet worshippers are expected to resonate with the expressions of those far removed from contemporary life.

Nonetheless, wrestling with words like "sin," "Lord," "salvation," and "grace" have helped us to better articulate our understandings of human nature, the power of God, and the different ways in which believers of different cultures have come to experience a life-giving and affirming faith. For example, some of the newer hymnals that seek greater inclusivity in language have summarily removed the word "Lord" from all lyrics. While that may please those who have negative associations with the term, there are some who are grateful that their Master and Lord is one of Love, giving a liberating identity to a traditionally oppressive societal role. While we strive to be open to new ways of depicting relationships and experiences with the Divine, we must heed the caution that simply abandoning those words that make us uncomfortable may, in turn, undermine the worship that deepens our own faith experience or enriches the experience and belief of another.

Rather than ignore them, let's unpack them and openly discuss their history, power, and limitations.

Paying Attention to Theological Terms

Make a list of theological terms that you or members of your congregation struggle with in hymns, prayers, or sermons because they make some people, perhaps yourself included, uncomfortable.

Choose one word on the list. Write a definition for the word without using words from the Bible or the Christian tradition. Use words from the everyday vernacular of the local culture in which you find yourself. The definition should be clear to those who are unchurched while being respectful of those who may embrace the traditional vocabulary.

Identify an illustration of the word from contemporary life, literature, movies, the environment, or the news.

> Repeat this exercise choosing vocabulary and an illustration that would be relevant for children and youth, while not being patronizing to adults.
>
> Consider how you might incorporate this language into a worship service.

Early on in my ministry, I learned that, rather than consider some words taboo, there is richness in bringing the words into the open and talking about them, even within the context of worship. Invariably, I and others are moved by the wisdom and experiences shared by worshippers when they are asked to reflect on how they have interpreted traditional language.

One wilderness walk I have taken with a congregation during Lent is a series of reflections on the "seven deadly sins."[6] In opening the series, I ask the congregation during worship, "If you were to shape your life and practice around a belief in 'original blessing' or 'original sin,' which would you choose and why?" I give them a moment of silence to consider the question, and then I open it up for sharing. If they're stuck, I may reword the question, "When you consider the way you live your life and your relationship with God, would you say you believe human beings are essentially good or essentially flawed?" The responses are wonderfully diverse, revealing much about people's faith, their life experiences, how they were raised, why they cling to one idea or the other, and the echoes of the conversation reverberate beyond the bounds of worship. Two young couples who "only came to church so our children would attend Sunday school" found themselves standing in the sanctuary, in a deep dialogue on the topic at hand, long after others had departed. In another community, one woman, after a long litany of voices claiming faith in original blessing, was courageous enough to stand alone and say that she thought "original sin" was formative in her life; it wasn't until the conversations unfolded in coffee hour that it became clear she was not alone.

In the weeks that followed, we considered anger, greed, envy, sloth, and pride. The reflection on pride was a conversational one as well. Some of the prompts included:

- What is pride?

---

6. While there are numerous resources for this topic, I have used the Seven Deadly Sins series published by Oxford University Press, 2003–2006.

Attending to the Language of Worship: Words

- When is pride a virtue?
- Why do you think pride would be included in a list of the seven deadly sins?
- Where do you see pride or a lack of pride, for better or worse, at play in this parable of the Pharisee and the tax collector (Luke 18:9–14 was the scripture reading for the day)?
- When is group pride a good thing?
- How do we know when group pride is no longer positive but instead sinful, separate from the goals of a good and loving God?
- How might the group pride of this local church serve us well?
- How might the pride in the traditions or buildings of this church trip us up?

The balance of the liturgy for these Sundays reflected the emotional and practical challenges of living with the light and shadow sides of the seven deadlies. Words that worshippers may have previously dismissed out of hand took on new significance in understanding their own identity and faith, opening them to new experiences of the Holy in the ordinary.

> *Guiding the Congregation's Attention to Traditional Theological Terms*
>
> Considering your experience with the congregation for which you plan worship, select one of the terms you wrote down in the previous exercise about paying attention to theological terms. It may be a word that your community avoids using or a term that has been debated from time to time.
>
> One of the blessings of these conversations is that they can reveal how our thinking influences our experiences and how our experiences influence our thinking, so it is important to use conversational prompts that address both what the worshippers have *learned* about the word (embedded theology) and how they have *experienced* what the word represents. Devise a couple of questions for the congregation that may

uncover what they believe about the concept you've chosen and how they have experienced or witnessed it in their lives.

You may ask them what Bible stories come to mind when they think of the word you have chosen, but be gentle. Don't pressure them. Assure them that there are no right or wrong answers and believe that yourself. Allow the conversation to grow organically without being shaped by your own agenda.

In your worship planning, identify a scripture passage that you will reflect upon either as part of the conversation with the congregation or in a sermon that follows the conversation.

Using the material you cultivated around this word in the previous exercise, incorporate the experiential language in the prayers throughout the service, remembering to consistently lift up how the goodness, grace, and love of God meet us in the experience.

The Blessing and Limitation of Borrowed Words

Discomfort with the theological terms and creedal debates that have defined much of the spoken language of the Christian tradition leads to liturgies that are shaped by words and ideas that are less than compelling for worshippers who long to be moved in a way that draws them into a closer relationship with God. Thankfully, there are many bridge builders among us who have published abundant resources for worship planners and leaders wanting to refresh liturgies with relevance and beauty in the twenty-first century. When we are looking for new vocabulary or metaphors for prayers or even sermons, grounded in the stories of the Bible or the truths and values of our tradition or denomination, we can find them. Bookstores and search engines will usher you to your favorite voices and introduce you to many more. Connecting with these resources is worth at least half the price of admission to ministry conferences and annual meetings.

At the same time, while there are faith-filled prayers catalogued through the generations of the Christian tradition, and it is good and right to carry those voices into the experience of worship on occasion, it is also important for worshippers to hear the struggles and celebrations from their daily lives, their church community, their town, the news of world from that week, or the seasonal signs caused by their geographic location reflected in the liturgy.

Both as a means of creating space for the worshippers to center themselves in the space and spirit of worship, as well as a way of making the traditional prayer of confession and assurance of pardon more active and meaningful for the participants, I often write a piece of the liturgy entitled "Centering Ourselves in the Generosity and Forgiveness of God." Centering ourselves in generosity is an opportunity to reflect upon our blessings and thanksgivings. The guidance I give the worshippers may focus on a specific context in which to identify blessings or it may be a more general prompt. After leaving a period of silence for the Spirit to lead the worshipper into the Gratefulness that is God within us, I offer the invitation to consider those relationships and experiences in our lives thirsting for reconciliation, second chances, or healing through forgiveness. In both parts of the centering meditation, I strive to use or elicit images or experiences that will emotionally engage the worshipper. The time of reflection has the deliberate and gentle pace of a guided meditation. It is typically closed with words assuring the worshippers of God's grace and the communal sharing of the Lord's Prayer, words that we can rely on in our thankfulness or our repentance when we may struggle in knowing how to approach God in prayer.

> *Centering Ourselves in the Generosity and Forgiveness of God: An Illustration*
>
> Some of us enter this space after a week that has held successes, accomplishments, love, beauty, enough money to do what we must and what we want, a great start to summer vacation, or a new beginning. For others of us, the week has held need in every direction we look. We've been surprised by diagnoses, wondered what we did to upset someone, or met with frustrating obstacles to getting to where we want to go.
>
> So that this sanctuary might pulse with praise and thanksgiving, take a moment to consider the blessings of your life this week or even just this morning. (Pause for silent reflection.)
>
> Distracted by our joy or by our pain, we may have made unfair judgments, said an unkind word, neglected to extend ourselves toward reconciliation as we justify our position, or

> been more inclined to indulge than to give. This moment is a gift to acknowledge those ways in which we have wandered from the path of Love and Grace. (Pause for silent reflection.)
>
> Only when we recognize having lost our way can we exercise the possibility of changing our course, seeking the trail that leads toward the Healing and Hope that is God. Choice, change, healing, hope—these are the assurances of a generous and forgiving God.
>
> Grateful and redeemed, or seeking to be so, we echo the prayer that Jesus taught us, using our own words...
>
> (See Appendix 2 for additional illustrations of "Centering Ourselves in the Generosity and Forgiveness of God.")

Another borrowed piece of the Christian tradition that I have often adapted in an effort to meet the worshippers in their life experience is the call and response in which the leader says, "God is good," and the congregation responds, "all the time." Then the leader says, "All the time," and the congregation responds, "God is good." The worship leader can simply use this call and response as is, repeating it a few times to imprint the truth it proclaims on the hearts of the participants, as well as to reap the blessings of an energetic, hope-filled communal chorus. With the intention of connecting the awareness of God's abiding Goodness to the experiences of daily life—however mundane, joyful, or tragic—I will insert relevant images or experiences into the call and response. It may be used as a call to worship or to bookend a spoken reflection.

> *God is Good ... All the Time: An Illustration*
>
> *God is good ... all the time. All the time ... God is good. God is good ... all the time.*
> When we are on our best behavior
> When we talk the talk and walk the walk of the gospel
> When we count ourselves among the blessed in The Beatitudes

Attending to the Language of Worship: Words

When we fall in with the righteous sheep, the good soil, and the perfect balance of Mary and Martha
God is good . . . all the time. All the time . . . God is good.
When we misspeak, misbehave, or misunderstand
When we fall off the wagon, go back on our word, or don't give our best effort
When we skip church, skip class, or skip a family gathering so we can enjoy a freshly fallen snow
When we hold company with the betraying Judas, the adulteress woman, the tax collectors, or the responsibility-shirking Pontius Pilate
And, yes, even when something really horrible happens
God is good . . . all the time. All the time . . . God is good.

Paying Attention to Borrowed Prayers in the Weekly Liturgy

Consider the pieces of your weekly liturgy that you often borrow from other resources or traditional prayers that you have omitted from your weekly worship service because they make you or your parishioners uncomfortable.

Call on the Spirit, and try writing your own version that prayer. You might find prayerfully moving through these steps helpful.

1. Identify the purpose of the prayer.
2. Make a list of the images and experiences that may illustrate or inform that purpose. The images and experiences may come from your daily life or may be related to the theme of a particular worship service. Be specific. For example, when directing the worshippers to Gratitude, list things for which you have been grateful in recent days. When encouraging a posture of repentance, name the struggles you've had with offending or being offended. The worshippers don't need to know these experiences come from your life, but you can rest assured that some

> will resonate with them, and their own experiences will pour into their hearts and minds.
>
> 3. Write the prayer in your own words. Try not to tell the worshipper how they *should* feel or what they *should* think. Simply lift up the images or experiences, and let them feel or think their way into the prayer themselves. God will meet them there, if you give them the space.

In addition to the standards that we return to time and time again in our weekly worship liturgy, there are the denominational resources that offer structure and substance for the occasional services of weddings, funerals, interments, and ordinations. Most liturgies for funerals or memorial services in the tradition of the United Church of Christ and other denominations begin with scripture assuring the gathered community of God's abiding presence. To simply say that God is present will find resonance in the hearts of some. For others, it will be white noise. It's what is said at funerals, but it doesn't ring true for them. While reading the Twenty-Third Psalm will be the balm of Gilead for some, for others it may be perceived as the rote recitation of impressionable, unquestioning believers. In an effort to comfort and teach, rather than solely relying on the imagery of the psalm, I expand the image of God's abiding presence to include an experience to which I am confident the listener can relate.

> *Opening Words at a Funeral: An Illustration*
>
> Reading: Psalm 23
>
> Some of us may be comforted when we hear the words of the psalmist assuring us that God is always present; a source of strength; a helping, even saving, hand in time of trouble; a voice of wisdom, guidance, love, and hope when we most need it. Others of us may be quite certain we've never heard the voice of God. As long as we have to suffer through the real certainties of death, disasters, and illnesses without cures, there can't possibly be a God.

Attending to the Language of Worship: Words

I invite you to look around you. Take in this vision of community: a diverse group of people drawn together by the life and death of one human being. A gathering of individuals who will be eager to listen to a stranger tell a story of remembrance; individuals who will offer a stranger a tissue to dry a tear of grief; individuals who will hold up a stranger who is weakened in sadness by offering an arm, a song, a smile, or a seat. This gathering of individuals is a visible reminder that the family, friends, and acquaintances of "Michael" are not alone in their loneliness for the one they love. I'm not sure what God's voice sounds like to others who have heard it, but this gathering is God incarnate as Strength, as Help in a time of loss, as Love and Hope, Comfort and Safety, Gratitude, and even Joy. If you experience any of these things in this brief moment of remembrance and thanksgiving, you have heard and seen God.

(See Appendix 3 for additional illustrations of prayers written for end-of-life services.)

Paying Attention to Borrowed Prayers in Occasional Services

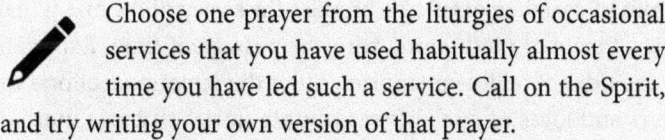

Choose one prayer from the liturgies of occasional services that you have used habitually almost every time you have led such a service. Call on the Spirit, and try writing your own version of that prayer.

1. Identify the purpose of the prayer. Keep in mind that attendees at special services may not be familiar with the rituals, beliefs, or language of your tradition. Your prayers may help those visitors understand why believers gather for this ritual and how they may see God in it.

2. Make a list of the images and experiences that may illustrate or inform that purpose. Consider choosing a metaphor that might be relevant to the person or persons for whom the service is being prepared, and identify how the

> promise or presence of God as well as the gathered community may be represented in that metaphor.
>
> 3. Write the prayer in your own words. Once again, try not to tell the worshipper how they *should* feel or what they *should* think. Simply lift up the images, and let them feel or think their way into the prayer themselves. God will meet them there, if you give them the space.

Maintaining the Connection to the Essential Gospel

Even as we dare to enter the sandbox with the academics and theologians, expanding the lexicon of our Christian faith and worship, we must do so with care so as not to lose the threads of experience and testimony that have woven generations together for millennia. Daniel Mendelsohn is the author of *Lost: A Search for Six of Six Million*, a story that tells of his quest to learn more about just six members of his extended family who experienced the Holocaust. Years after publishing the book, when he speaks of wading through both primary and secondary, written and oral sources for his research, he offers a bit of wisdom about the record of history. It is one reason why he wanted to pursue his family's story, and it is also why there will always be a limit to what he can know to be true. The greater the distance in time from the original event, the broader the sweep of the brush that paints the story. Pieces of truth erode with the passage of time. Experiences are lost to the tides of fallible memories, if not the intentional efforts to forget. The scars and loves of one's life reassemble stories that rest more easily in their hearts. And there is the practical reality that the story needs to be compressed and summarized as history accumulates.

The global Christian community has a history of debating the words and concepts of the faith. The tradition is defined, in part, by those very differences. We must be careful that the linguistic tug-of-wars and the effort to open the door to the fresh understandings of contemporary disciples do not ultimately distance us from the essential gospel. Those whose impression of the Christian church in the twenty-first century is one of hierarchy, intolerance, and exclusion are testifying to the prevailing message of the human experience of the historical church. Mired in history, they have missed the essential truth that God is Love, God is Good, God is bigger than the details

Attending to the Language of Worship: Words

over which we worry or weep. No matter what the challenge or the celebration, the question or the revelation, the debate or the resolution, worship leaders and planners must use care not to lose that truth as we design the rooms in God's mansion to suit our own tastes or, in this context, as we prepare a worship service that is intended to carry believers and doubters to the reassuring experience of an abiding, still-speaking God.

After two decades of planning and leading worship with vigilant attentiveness to words, stories, and metaphors, I felt I had mastered the use of language in creating the space for worshippers to be poised for transformative spiritual experiences with God. I had witnessed the spiritual life of individuals and communities take new flight as they recognized God in the midst of their living, their worship, and their ministry. They found their voice in testimony, spiritual reflection, and community decision making. Their relationships with God and one another grew more intimate. It was then that I realized that the language of worship is much more than words, and I had only begun to till the soil of the worship experience, sowing seeds of God-encounters that may be felt even before they are understood.

3

Attending to the Language of Worship: Music

> *Paying Attention to Worship Music*
>
> Take a few minutes to write about how the music offered in your weekly worship service makes you feel and why?

Musical Offerings

HAVING WORSHIPPED IN A variety of congregations in the United Church of Christ as well as other traditions, I'm fairly confident most responses to this question fall into one of three categories: Great Performances, Doing the Best We Can with What We've Got, and Invaluable Orchestration Partner.

Great Performances

There are churches that rely on their music ministry to attract new members, to keep current worship attendees happy, and to add the necessary flourish to the festival services of the "high holy days." They pull out all the stops for Music Sunday, Easter, or Christmas, and there is always extra publicity for those Sundays when something "special" is happening with music. The choir members love to "perform" for the "audience." Church members boast about being "known for their music." The music is often

Attending to the Language of Worship: Music

wonderfully presented—moving, entertaining—and provides something safe and satisfying to talk about following worship or whenever the topic of church comes up, more often in the shape of a critic's rave review than testimony of a transformative God-encounter. And let me say, thanks be to God for the passion of the musicians and for the musical interludes that may, in and of themselves, be the thresholds over which worshippers walk into profound spiritual experience.

Doing the Best We Can with What We've Got

Somewhere on the opposite end of the spectrum, there are those churches whose rhythms within the worship service or throughout the liturgical year don't vary much from one Sunday to the next. If they have a choir, it is fledgling or diminishing. Decision-making about the music is an occasional delicate dance or a never-ending wrestling match between the lead musician and the pastor, as the lead musician often outweighs the pastor in years of service by decades, and the two may have very different aspirations for the role and substance of music in the worship service. Music choices are often based upon competencies and personal preferences rather than strategic planning in accordance with a vision of the whole worship experience. And let me say, thanks be to God for the dedication of those who ensure that there is music in worship, no matter the degree of organization or excellence. If offered for the glory of God, it has its place in drawing worshippers into communion with one another and with the Holy One of Blessing.

Invaluable Orchestration Partner

Some may speak of churches whose music is an integral part of the whole, no matter the size of the choir, the number of instruments, or the credentials of the lead musician. Music leads the worshippers in and out of the stories being told, the sacraments being celebrated, and the prayers being lifted up. All worship leaders are working together to direct (or orchestrate) the attention of the worshippers in a way that ushers them through an emotional experience in concert with the scripture message and ritual of the worship service. Singing is invitational. Those gathered are welcome to sing as the Spirit moves them, whether it's a hymn or an anthem, an interlude or a postlude. Music sometimes punctuates and other times carries the message or movement of the day. And may I express deep gratitude to God for the ministries of music that partner with ministries of word and ritual to create a cohesive context for engaging hearts and minds in the exercise of thanks and praise that is worship, with the hopeful potential of creating the space for God-encounters that change lives.

The difference between music ministries that are either Great Performances or Doing the Best with What We've Got and those that are Invaluable Orchestration Partners is the degree to which the worshipper may remain engrossed in the emotional experience and reflection of worship rather than fighting the distraction of thinking about the ministry of music as an entity in and of itself. It is not a question of the quality of the musical offering, whether splendid or meager. The problem is the disconnect between the fundamental purpose of creating a worshipful experience and the music that is being offered in that context. Whether the congregation is transported to the concert hall (Great Performances) or to the concerns about the organist voiced at the music committee meeting (Doing the Best with What We've Got), the music has shifted the worshippers' focus from the worship experience to the music itself.

If worship planners and leaders want to guide their worshipping congregations into transformative spiritual experiences, and if we understand such divine recalibration to be couched in emotional experiences more times than not, we would be well served to understand the prominent role music plays in this process. After spending twenty years expanding the verbal lexicon of Christian worship, with the hope that the words I and others used might elicit a change of heart in worship participants by tapping into their emotional experience, I have learned that music is as critical as the words of prayer, story, testimony, belief, and practice. Music, not words, is the primary language of the human experience. It was and is both the first mode of communication of human beings as well as the most impulsive, least controlled expression of feeling.

In the context of worship, melodies, harmonies, rhythm, and tone will build or dismantle the altar at which worshippers might lay their deepest grief, their most profound need, or their highest praise and thanksgiving.

Attending to the Language of Worship: Music

> *Paying Attention to What Worship Music Communicates*
>
> ✏️ Consider the music of a recent worship service that you have led or attended. If you have a copy of the order of worship, take a moment to review it. How and what would you say that the music communicated to the worshippers? How did it connect with the rest of the worship experience?

A Valuable Link between Science and Faith Experience

The Wailing Wall. A delicious bite of food. A happy baby waking in a crib. An ice cube down the shirt. A mouse under foot. Sex. Touching something very hot. Watching fireworks. A hammer hitting a finger. Stepping out into a cold winter morning when you don't have enough layers on. Walking into a room that smells of your favorite meal. A thumb-sucking toddler. A sung benediction. We've made the music. We've heard the music. We've felt the music. We "sing" from raw emotion, and we make music, often times without thought. Musical key and notes may be elusive, but how we feel is often plainly clear.

Music grew out of our most primitive verbalizations. Before we humans were writing music, we were verbalizing all kinds of melodies—melodies that captured fear, comfort, awe, joy, and loss. Jaak Panksepp, one of the founders of the brain science of emotion, suggests that "music is the most sophisticated human 'language' of emotions . . ." because the sound that many call music today, which is created by composers and lyricists, uses raw emotional sounds as its building blocks.[1] Before we could cognitively place notes of different shapes on the musical staff, melodies took flight from synapses firing deep within our brain. Emotions are the raw impulsive responses to external stimuli. Our spontaneous audible responses to those feelings are the pitches and cadences that have informed music throughout time. It follows that if we want to engage the worshipper on an emotional level, we must rely, in part, on the "language of emotions" to liberate the participant from a purely cognitive approach to worship.

---

1. Panksepp and Biven, *Archaeology of Mind*, 16.

Many worship leaders in my tradition center the substance of their worship service on the intellect. The sermon is a time to teach or convince or justify. The prayers are a time to speak to the latest news, in the neighborhood or the world. The worshippers consume worship in a top-down manner. The words go into the frontal lobe of the brain (known as the neocortex), they are considered, meaning is attached to them, and they are digested. Listeners keep what is nourishing, and the rest passes through. They may leave the sanctuary having *learned* something *about* God, themselves, or the theme of the day. While such messages may be enlightening and relevant, a worship experience that helps worshippers feel God's presence must go beyond the intellectual.

When we embrace music as an essential, substantive language of the whole worship experience, we reach down to where the hairs stand up on the back of the neck. We tap into another part of the brain, called the subcortex, where emotions are engaged or awakened, and worshippers may *feel* their way into an *experience* of God. Worshippers then thoughtfully reflect upon that experience on their way to articulating belief.

> *Paying Attention to Music that Moves You*
>
> Take some time to reflect on music that has moved you. What are some of your favorite songs or other pieces of music, regardless of genre? How do they make you feel? Why do you respond this way? If you were to create a soundtrack for your favorite scripture passage, what music would you choose and why?

Increasingly, brain scientists are identifying how music can transform our emotional being, unlock our cognitive dissonance, and move us in ways that words and gestures may not. As creatively as we may try to engage a person's emotional experience with verbal description, deconstructed metaphors, and dramatic storytelling, the effective use of music in reflecting or illustrating the invitation of the day can carry worshippers to the transformative thin places of vulnerable or joyful communion with God and one another, with no cognitive deliberation on the part of the listener.

Awareness of the role of music is not typically lost on the two anchors of the Christian liturgical calendar—birth and resurrection. Many pastors and parishioners have debated whether or not Christmas carols should be sung during the worship services of Advent because, on the one hand, the feelings associated with the Advent wait are lost if we fast forward to the celebration of the birth. On the other hand, doesn't singing carols throughout the commercial and social whirlwind leading to Christmas remind us of "the reason for the season" and soothe us in our "happy place"? Most leaders and followers agree that the lamenting music of Maundy Thursday and Good Friday is necessarily different from the festival music of Easter because we are on a journey from the heart-wrenching passion to the miraculous resurrection. But what happens when the shift in story and mood isn't so obvious?

What happens when we look to music as a partner in guiding the worship experience throughout the balance of the year? The strategic singing of "Silent Night" on Christmas Eve or "Were You There" during Holy Week often moves worshippers to that thin place of a heartfelt God-encounter. So too, a music ministry that is an Invaluable Orchestration Partner helps to *unlock* the emotional experience of the gathered community as well as *synchronize* that emotional experience with the stories unfolding within individuals, the community, the worship service, and the world outside the walls of the sanctuary. Music is both a means of escorting the human mind and spirit *to a different place* and a way of *meeting* a person *in the moment*. Both intentions require the worship planners to be mindful of the thoughts, feelings, and experiences that worshippers may carry with them into the space of worship.[2]

---

2. Thomas Merton is known for cultivating his relationship with God through contemplation. In his book *The Inner Experience*, he reflects on his journey from an understanding of contemplation as a compartmentalized activity in his monastic practice to the idea of living a sustained contemplative life. He identifies that a requisite step in discovering a meaningful connection with God is to first take stock of and unify one's own "inner life." As we make our way in the world, we can find ourselves stretched in many different directions, being many things to many people for better or for worse, while also strategizing the pursuit of our own fulfillment. Our rhythms may not sync with the rhythms of the world in any given moment, so we will at times play the role expected of us while we would much prefer to hold another thought, offer another response, or engage in another activity. The authentic self soon falls prey to the widening gap between the inner reality and the outward manifestation of our existence. We become "fragmented." In the privacy of our own being, there is a necessity for congruence. Whether endeavoring to live a contemplative life or planning a worship service, one goal is to create the space for the holy moment of discovering one's own incongruence and a hope for recalibration, however simple or profound.

Music Ministry as Invaluable Orchestration Partner: Illustrations

Meeting Anxiety with Comfort

It was my first Sunday leading worship as interim minister in a new community. I knew there would be anxiety in the hearts of individuals and in the system of the congregation. It was a time of change, grief, fear, and hope. For the introit, I sang a few lines from "Getting to Know You." I started in the back of the sanctuary, walking up and down the aisles, greeting people with my facial expressions, smiling as I heard others let out a warm chuckle of surprise or welcome and begin to hum along. This friendly and relaxing opening was only the beginning. Rather than the usual "introduction sermon," which can have worshippers sitting on the edge of their pews listening intently for the "wrong" word or a push for a dreaded change, we spent a good part of the service just singing together—and not just hymns of my choosing, as I wanted to learn more about the hymns that this community cherished. It was a "Worshipper's Choice" Sunday. We opened and closed the service singing a number of hymns chosen by those gathered. As some may have felt the anxiety of change happening beyond their control, I gave them an opportunity to exercise their voice, in more ways than one. At the end of the service, I could almost hear and feel the congregation exhale, having discovered a spot of shared common ground upon which to enter into a new relationship. Thanks be to God.

Waiting on the Spirit's Bidding

There may be circumstances in the congregation or the wider community that have caused heartbreak, conflict, or a division between "winners" and "losers." With the hope that those gathered for worship may find welcome, affirmation, and sanctuary in the space of worship, I choose a brief hymn or borrow a Taizé chant and invite worshippers to sing, hum, or

> just listen as the Spirit moves them. We repeat it several times. Coming together in a shared rhythm builds community and helps us to center ourselves for the worship at hand or equip ourselves with a rhythm that steadies us as we return to our daily lives. Thanks be to God.
>
> ## Walking Music
>
> Children may be coming forward for a children's message or being dismissed to Sunday school. It may be time for the elements of the Lord's Supper to be shared, the offering to be collected, the gifts to be brought forward, the candles to be lit or extinguished. Worship leaders and participants move about the sanctuary throughout the worship service. While there is certainly a time for intentional silent reflection during those moments of the worship experience when those gathered are not just waiting for the next piece of the liturgy to unfold, the necessary movement in a worship service can be disruptive to the emotional flow of the experience. In an effort to hold the worshippers' attention in the emotional space that is intended, I will ask the musician to play appropriate music underneath the activity. Consciously or otherwise, those who are moving as well as those watching them move are guided by a shared rhythm intentionally set by the worship planners, reinforcing the worshipful context in which the movement occurs. Thanks be to God.

If you go to a professional baseball game, you may find yourself dancing in your seat throughout the game. It happens to me at Fenway Park. Each time a Red Sox player approaches the batter box, his stride is accompanied by music he has requested to be played through the stadium speakers. If you watch the Olympics, you'll see many competitors listening to music as they prepare for their time in the spotlight. The music orients them to the task before them in a way that is inspiring, energizing, or relaxing—helping them to focus their physical and mental attention in a way that will lead them to success or victory. It is not a happy accident. It is not simply because younger generations actually focus better if they have multiple stimuli in the background of their primary activity. It is because music generates particular responses in one's body, mind, and spirit.

If the worship planners and leaders are vested with the responsibility of guiding the gathered community into a worship experience that is heartfelt and spiritually renewing, the decision makers need to support that effort with a ministry of music that is an integral piece of the whole. When worship preparation has intention and cohesion, the music of the service is a critical partner in creating the space for a change of heart that may be recognized as a visceral connection with a Power Greater than Ourselves.

Music as Distraction

Too often the ministry of music is separated from the balance of the worship planning. Perhaps the pastor shares the scripture passage and the sermon theme with the lead musician in advance, or perhaps not. The pastor may be responsible for selecting hymns, without knowing the ability of the choir or congregation to sing chosen arrangements, which forces participants to a thinking place of trying to figure out notes and rhythms rather than prayerfully singing their way into communion and community.

Many congregations are also trapped in the idea that only certain types of music are appropriate in church and that special music is only needed on certain days. There are unwritten rules about classical versus contemporary music choices, which often result in reserving popular or playful music for "Youth Sunday." Trumpets play on Jazz Sunday and Easter. Music from different cultures makes an appearance on World Communion Sunday, and perhaps Pentecost. Spirituals echo in sanctuaries throughout Black History Month.

The lead musicians may select music based upon who is going to be singing in the choir on a given Sunday or which masterpiece they have worked diligently to prepare or what has been requested by a persistent member of the congregation, which results in the music harshly interrupting the tone for the service that the pastor or others have worked diligently to create, even if the musicians "did a wonderful job." Hence, worshippers may have been ushered to the threshold of a particular emotional encounter with the Spirit—perhaps a glimpse of Holy Light in the midst of a contemplative Lenten wilderness walk—and then the community is suddenly redirected by the strains of a merry lilt or a toe-tapping bluegrass number.

Attending to the Language of Worship: Music

In the same way, "Great Performances" choirs often draw more attention to themselves than to the emotional space their offering should be creating so that they or others might be surprised by an encounter with God. In fact, often they are so focused on the "audience" that they lose touch with the fact that they, too, are part of the congregation experiencing the power of the music in communion with, not separate from, the other worshippers.

"Doing the Best We Can with What We've Got" choirs refuse to admit when their valiant but meager efforts are distracting the congregation from the experience of worship. Rather than losing themselves in the emotional flow of the worship, congregants detour to thoughts about the health of the church or the conflicts in the choir.

There is absolutely a place in worship for those who want to lift up their voices or their musical instrumentation for God's glory, no matter what their skill level, but we lose our way when the only thing we expect from our music ministry is applause for a job well done or when we shirk our leadership responsibility by telling ourselves that we're doing a good deed by letting someone "play on" when it's long past time for retirement. Asking a performance choir to consider God before perfect pitch or ushering out the old so there is room for new growth are challenging conversations that require gentleness and reverence, but they are necessary if musicians are to understand and embrace their proper role in worship.

Musicians as Worship Leaders

There is a verse in the Gospel of John that has been omitted from many translations of the Bible. "For an angel of the Lord went down at certain seasons into the pool and stirred up the water: whoever stepped in first after the stirring of the water was made well from whatever disease that person had" (John 5:4). While singing in the choir or playing an instrument may be a personally joyful, fulfilling experience or a spiritual discipline for those who sing or play, musicians are also worship leaders for the gathered congregation. All those who preach, pray, sing, and play hold the potential of being the angels that stir (or trouble) the water that moves worshippers to experience emotional, spiritual, or physical healing and wholeness.

One way to affect change in the music ministry of the worshipping community is to foster greater awareness of the weighty role music plays in the experience of a worship service leading to the transformation of individual and communal souls that many worshippers yearn for. Rather than leaving the pastor, the worship team, and the lead musician to their own devices, the congregation would be well served by having at least a core group of participants who have an understanding of and commitment to the liturgical purpose of worship music. Such awareness impacts the church budget, the use and care of the sanctuary space, as well as the worship experience.

One way to foster this understanding is through a music retreat. Though the retreat may be geared toward choir members, lead musicians, music and worship team members, deacons, and other decision makers, the invitation could be extended to others as well. The goal is to lead participants into experiences that illustrate music as a primitive and contemporary soundtrack of emotion, which has the power to build or dismantle the worship space where humans hope to meet the Holy. Chants, song, prayer, and ritual are used throughout the retreat to carry the group members into connections with God and with one another, as well as to provide a sacred, reflective pause between activities. Exercises may include the following:

> *Guiding the Congregation's Attention to*
> *Music as a Language for Worship*
>
> ON THE LIGHTER SIDE
>
> These prompts are a fun way of helping worship musicians and others discover that music grew out of our most primitive verbalizations. Before we humans were writing music, we were verbalizing all kinds of melodies. Composing came from these audible expressions. We aren't born knowing what certain experiences and emotions sound like. It is something we learn just by living life and listening. Musicians then try to replicate these audible experiences through music in order to move people.
>
> Prompt 1: Take a moment in silence to think about a sound that evokes a strong feeling in you (for example, the rolling of an ocean tide, the siren of a fire engine, or the slam of a door). After a period of silence, invite the participants to share with one another.

Attending to the Language of Worship: Music

Prompt 2: Take a few moments in silence to make a list of experiences that trigger an audible response (for example, a delicious bite of food, fireworks, the smell of sour milk, stubbing one's toe, or moving an aching body). After a period of silence, invite participants to name one experience at a time. The rest of the group responds by making the sound triggered by the experience.

A Way into Reflecting upon the Ministry of Music

Listen: Play excerpts from a variety of genres of music and ask the participants to record (in three words or fewer) how the music makes them feel. Music genres may include drumming, classical sacred music, congregational hymn singing during different times in the Christian liturgical year (include strong choral singing and weak choral singing), African songs, mass choir, organ, piano, orchestral, recorders, contemporary arrangements of traditional hymns, and secular popular music.

Discuss: Invite participants to share the feeling responses they recorded while listening. Then facilitate discussion using the following prompts or others that rise up for you:

How does the spectrum of emotions you recorded relate to the spectrum of emotions evoked in the music ministry of your weekly worship service?

How does the music for the weekly worship service get selected? Is the person selecting the music aware of the desired movement of the service?

If, as leaders, you are attempting to move the worshippers in a certain direction, how does music help or hinder that movement?

What are the challenges to maintaining a music ministry that supports the emotional flow of the worship service?

Some congregations may have a musician who is gifted in improvisational music. I have been blessed to be a part of a couple different communities in which there is a musician who can play music in response to particular prayer requests. As part of an evening prayer (and music) service, the musician invites worshippers to share a feeling or experience that they want to hold up before God, and the musician improvises several bars of music as accompaniment to laying that feeling or experience on the altar of a listening God. If you have such a musician in your midst, another exercise for the retreat may look like this. Choose six Bible stories that may be familiar to the participants. The tone or drama of the stories should vary. Number the stories one through six. Ask the musician to choose a story and, without saying which story he or she is playing, tell the story just using the instrument (piano, organ, guitar). The participants then guess which story is being told through the music being played. It's another fun illustration of how music converses with our emotional and experiential lives. As Joan Chittister says, "There is music in the cosmos, music in the sea, music in the wind, music untrammeled and untrapped in the human heart. Releasing it within ourselves is a first step on the way to a soaring spiritual life."[3]

Music "soothes the savage breast," is "the food of love," "the shorthand of emotion," and "the language of the spirit," as great writers have noted. Worship leaders need to harness that power. For when the hair stands up on the back of the neck, when worshippers are moved to tears, or hope-filled laughter interrupts despair even for a moment, epiphany rises up to meet us. God is felt, faith is nurtured, lives are transformed, and communities are strengthened—all for the good.

---

3. Chittister, *Listen with the Heart*, 87.

4

Attending to the Language of Worship: Symbols and Ritual

While there have been stained glass windows, elaborate stone masonry, and liturgical art in the various places where I have led worship, most sanctuaries are a product of the Protestant Reformation. They are simple. There is a Communion table, not an altar. There is a baptismal font that is portable, so it can be tucked away and brought to the fore at the appropriate time. The cross is empty. There are no icons telling the story of Jesus' life, death, and resurrection, or liturgical art depicting saints. The recalibration brought about through the Reformation included setting aside faith objects and reclaiming the primacy of the Word. Beyond the symbols and rituals of the sacraments, the language of the Protestant worship experience centers on words and music. So it is still.

In the last chapter, we acknowledged that music has the power to communicate something to us without our conscious engagement. Words, however, are more complicated because they require cognitive processing, which can be hindered in all sorts of ways: a wandering mind, a lack of comprehension, fatigue, an orientation toward debate, to name a few. In addition, we are all wired differently. Some of us see things best with words, others with music or pictures or objects, and others with bodily gestures. Some of us need quiet, solitary time to process an idea, while others like to "throw it out to the group" and draw from the cacophony of a brainstorming session.

Putting the bountiful and boundless experience of God into the small container of the spoken word leaves too much on the table, unable to be consolidated and packaged into our limited vocabulary. Consequently, I have often taken a page from the educators who embrace the idea of multiple intelligences, the proposition that different individuals learn most effectively using different modes of processing: visual, bodily, musical, interpersonal (extrovert), intrapersonal (introvert), lingual, or logical.[1] Such a variety in the ways we communicate, especially around emotional experiences, is apparent when you consider the response to tragedies that traumatize a city, a region, or a nation. When those who are affected need or want to respond, we read faith testimonies in 280-character tweets; tell stories with photos on Instagram or Facebook; hold prayer vigils and rallies; build memorials with objects; compose songs, prayers, poetry, and dances; or organize for grassroots activism. So too, the elusive magnitude of the experience of God requires us to rely on more than the window of words to catch a glimpse or display a vision of the Divine in the experience of worship. Sometimes symbols and ritual are the artwork of belief. Other times they are the windows to seeing God.

Symbols as Definition of Sacred Space

Paying Attention to Symbols in the Worship Experience

Reflect upon the various worship spaces of your spiritual journey. You may want to close your eyes and visualize those spaces or take some time to sit in your current worship space. What are the symbols in the space that have been integral to your worship experience? Why? Using pen and paper, depict those symbols with words or sketches and note their importance to you.

---

1. In *Frames of Mind*, first published in 1983, Howard Gardner suggests there are eight ways that people learn best. And for each learning style he identifies how the person thinks, what the person loves, and what the person needs to optimize learning. For example, people who are verbal-linguistic think in words; they love reading, writing, telling stories, and playing word games; and they learn best by using books, tapes, writing tools, dialogue, discussion, debate, and stories. People who are spatial learners think in images and pictures, while logical-mathematical learners think by reasoning, using numbers, and logic. Others may think and learn best through music or through contact with the outdoors and objects in nature or through movement.

Attending to the Language of Worship: Symbols and Ritual

The simplicity of the sanctuary is respected in the places where I lead worship, but that doesn't mean that the visual presentations that define the space are not part of my weekly worship planning. The consideration of the space begins with what is already there. Whenever I begin a ministry in a new location, I take time to become familiar with the worshipping space. I walk about the space, open doors and drawers, read plaques, and ask questions to elicit stories. "Tell me about this Communion set. Where did it come from? Why is it important to you?" "Who made this banner?" "Tell me why you have chosen to put these particular things in the narthex." "How long has the choir sung from that space? Is it a good space for the choir?" "Who decided which flags belong in the sanctuary?" Asking the questions and inviting the stories help both the new pastor as well as long-time members reflect upon what their worship space and its objects communicate to those who cross the threshold.

Discovering the Unintended Markers of Sacred Space

I was one of the final two candidates for the position of pastor for a small rural church. I had already had two interviews with members of the search committee—one on the phone and one at a member's home. During this last interview, I would finally see the church space for the first time. I approached the front door of the church and saw that the welcome mat had been pushed aside and weeds were growing up through the spaces of the rope-woven rectangle. I went inside for the interview and a tour of the church space. The signs of neglect came in quick succession. All of the spaces that could hide things—behind the rail of the chancel, the former choir loft, the once-and-future children's space—were filled with items that may once have been purposeful, but were now piles of relics from worship services, repair jobs, donations, decorations, and ministries gone by. I pulled back a curtain in the parlor, where the congregation enjoyed coffee hour each week, and I discovered a hole that ran along the window casing and played host to a growing mushroom-like fungus.

I would eventually receive a call to serve this congregation. The only thing that gave me serious pause in my discernment was the obvious neglect of the physical space. How could a community walk by its own welcome mat every week and not notice or not care that it no longer welcomed people but had become a sign of indifference and a symbol of lack of attention? What did the overwhelming degree of clutter say about how this congregation valued its worship space? Was the stewardship of their physical space representative of their lack of intention around other aspects of their ministry—finances, relationships, liturgy, and invitation?

I would come to understand these unintended symbols as signs of a church with low self-esteem. It seems there is often a mentality in churches that they should make do with the least possible investment in their own upkeep and appearance. They often use everyone else's hand-me-downs, whether they are furniture, office supplies, computers, rugs, curtains, china, or decorations. In addition, they often save everything, trying to anticipate every future need, so they never have to buy anything new.

Low self-esteem is one reality that informs the markers that shape the sacred space housing worship. On the other end of the spectrum are the many symbols that are ego driven. How many times have you walked into a church and found walls covered in plaques? I admit that I am sensitive about plaques that are mounted to give honor to someone who has donated time or money in support of the church. As a pastor who tries to turn her own attention, as well as that of others, to the truth that all we have is a gift from God, I am bothered by the need that some churches have to put up a plaque for every contribution "of substance" from a "significant" donor. It implies that there is a scale for measuring the magnitude of gifts given, and it sets in motion an angst-ridden process of discerning what "deserves" a plaque and what does not. Does the widow's mite never deserve recognition? Furthermore, there is the danger of memorializing something that will ultimately be a fleeting expression of a certain time and place. Even worse is when these icons prevent the space from being updated to meet the needs of contemporary worship experiences and their august presence makes the congregation afraid to tamper with them. Antique fixtures, for example, don't allow for full and flexible lighting, and the maintenance of cleaning the brass and replacing the light bulbs often gets postponed far too long because it's too big of a job for anyone in the congregation to manage. It somehow is seen as more faithful to maintain a museum-like quality to the worship space rather than adapting it for an experience of worship that is alive, organic, fluid, flexible, and just more practical, especially for the visually challenged struggling to read the hymns. Banners and curtains are faded, tattered, outdated, and less appropriate for the space now than they were decades ago when a beloved matriarch of the community made a generous gift to the church, but disposing of them or repurposing them seems like an affront to the original donor.

Attending to the Language of Worship: Symbols and Ritual

It is true that some liturgical objects are integral to some worshippers' spiritual life and practice. Objects, fixtures, and dressings can be important signs and symbols that communicate a message and may be the apertures through which the gathered community claps their eyes on the Holy—a simple, hand-hewn cross with a deep patina, a church bell that has rung worshippers into church for centuries and announced momentous historical events to the town.

Surely, though, there are other items that could be tucked away and brought to the fore at the time of nostalgic celebrations, such as homecoming Sunday, anniversaries of the church's establishment, or All Saints' Day. To the long-time church members, these items may hold cherished memories; for others, they may be the white noise that parishioners have become accustomed to ignoring because they have no bearing on their worship experience. Alongside respecting the history testified to by the space and its objects, we need to consider what these symbols communicate to worshippers, old and new. Do they represent a community that is out of touch with the lives and spiritual needs of those beyond their walls—insular and seeking to preserve the past—or does the space reflect a community that is likely to welcome new people, new ideas, and new liturgical symbols and expressions?

It's important to be careful when taking stock of the intended and unintended markers of the sacred space that hosts worship. It is a spiritual exercise, and I believe it is best if, as pastor, I work to equip church members to engage in the exercise of discerning what stays and what gets set aside, stored, or repurposed. There will always be differences of experience and opinion regarding the liturgical, memorial, and practical objects that are part of the worship space. While everyone will not always agree on decisions made, it is worthwhile to involve the worship team or deacons or other leaders in the decision-making process and to offer a clear rationale as to why a particular decision was made. A church will be best served by fostering a culture that affirms the fluid nature of sacred objects and space.

*Guiding the Congregation's Attention to the
Symbols and Signs of the Worship Space*

Part 1

Gather in the sanctuary those who are responsible for designing and maintaining the worship space, from entry to exit. As an introduction to the idea of looking for signs that do not come in the form of words printed on paper, invite the group members to think of and then talk about the following:

signs of new life	signs of danger
signs of desperation	signs of health
signs of hope	signs of death

Place paper and pen in each public space that is involved in the weekly worship experience: the entryway into the sanctuary, the sanctuary, the exit from the sanctuary, the bathroom, and any other space through which a worshipper travels when attending worship. Working individually or in small groups, invite the participants to spend time in each space and list *all* of the signs and symbols in that space, indicating what those signs and symbols communicate to worship attendees.

The list should include those items that are intentionally placed in the space, as well as those that have just landed there. It should include those items that have positive, liturgical, or communal purpose, as well as those that communicate unintentional or negative messages. Consider, too, what the signs and symbols communicate to different audiences: long-time members; visitors; children; young adults; or those with visual, auditory, or mobility challenges.

After everyone has had a chance to engage all the spaces, invite participants to share their observations with the group. Collect the lists, collate the information, and file them for future use.

Attending to the Language of Worship: Symbols and Ritual

PART 2

Ask each participant to invite someone who is unfamiliar with the worship space to tour the space with the participant. The guest is asked to identify all signs and symbols that are part of the spaces through which the guest travels, indicating what those signs and symbols communicate to the guest. The tour guide makes a list of what is noticed.

The church group then reassembles and shares what they have learned. They combine the information gathered in the two sessions and consider what possible changes might be made to address the unintended or misguided signs and symbols in the worship space.

Symbols as the Artwork of Belief

Have you ever sat around a campfire, by a backyard firepit, or in front of a fireplace with briskly burning logs? There is something mesmerizing about watching the flames dance, something deeply spiritual in their paradoxical ever-changing constancy. One of the most joyful places of my childhood was the summer camp I attended each August. The heart of the camp was the campfire circle. We gathered on a circle of logs placed around the fire every night for singing and games. The fire burned well into the night, as the campers drifted off to sleep and the counselors who were on duty abided in the circle. After breakfast, the fire was reignited, providing a warming place for those who were coming out of their swimming lessons (and a crematorium for the leeches!). I loved camp, and I loved that fire. For me, fire has become one of my Spirit objects. My body, mind, and spirit are recalibrated toward the Holy when I focus my attention on a flame.

Similarly, ever since I read chapter 3 of *The Grapes of Wrath* by John Steinbeck, land turtles have had that same divine pull. The three-page chapter depicts a turtle that is absolutely and resolutely set on its mission—the journey across the highway. Push, pull, scratch, teeter, flip. It just keeps going, even in the face of one threat after another. There's the woman who drives too fast, with a lack of attention, yet a compassionate impulse causes her to avoid the turtle. And then there's the trucker who actually aims to hit and destroy the turtle. The reader gets so wrapped up in the turtle's perseverance and survival that it is easy to overlook the blessing that the turtle carried with him—one head of wild oats that is caught in its shell and that falls out on the other side of the road. There, as Steinbeck describes, "three of the spearhead seeds stuck in the ground. And as the turtle crawled on down the embankment, its shell dragged dirt over the seeds."[2] The turtle had forever changed the landscape of the earth and the environment of life in that place, planting seeds of new life.

I have one beautifully hand-carved wooden turtle that sits on my desk to remind me of the truth that even in the most difficult experiences we may carry blessings out of the wilderness moment, and they can seed new life. The turtle could be called a Spirit animal as it ushers me into communion with God.

> *Paying Attention to Spirit Objects and Animals*
>
> Beyond the traditional symbols of your Christian faith, is there an object or an animal that is an expression of a spiritual truth for you? Perhaps it is a piece of sea glass that illustrates how the repetitive ebb and flow of God's grace can smooth our rough edges. You may visit the same tree on your daily walk and admire its beauty and strength through the seasons and how it has adapted to thrive in its environment. What is or could be a Spirit object or animal for you? How does it provide a bridge to the Holy for you? Consider sharing your testimony in a worship service and inviting others to do the same.

All these images point to the power of the visual in worship planning. One of the first techniques I used to create the space for a transformative spiritual experience in worship was to be mindful of the visual representations that may illustrate the reflection for the day. Just as worship planners are often looking for new words and stories to express constant, enduring truths, so too might we offer new symbols or visual illustrations as the artwork of our belief.

2. Steinbeck, *Grapes of Wrath*, 22.

Attending to the Language of Worship: Symbols and Ritual

Open to Interpretation

Édouard Manet, *Fish (Still Life)*, **1864, oil, 73.5 x 92.4 cm**[3]

In looking at the picture above, the chef might see an adventure with different flavors, textures, techniques, and surprising outcomes. The wealthy hostess sees fresh, succulent extravagances that will be brought together to build a first course that pleases her guests. The struggling fisherman, with a family of six waiting at home, is grateful for a good day of fishing and harvesting that yielded enough to sell, so his family can eat simply and hope to make ends meet. The child who has grown up on the Midwestern plains, unfamiliar with sea life, makes a funny face and feels shivers through his body, as he is "grossed out" by the dead fish, a squiggly eel, and slimy oysters.

Paying Attention to a Still Life

 What do you see in this image? Where does it take you? How does it make you feel? Where is God or the Jesus story in this image?

A still life painting may elicit excitement, joy, comfort, discomfort, anticipation, or inspiration. It illustrates a story that we carry with us or a

3. Art Institute of Chicago, https://www.artic.edu/artworks/44892/fish-still-life.

story we wish to create. A trip to an art museum can be a journey through diverse earthly spaces, forgotten universal truths, memories and wonders as you stand in the halls of a singular building. In the same way, we can bring new symbols into the worship space to create the opportunity for attaching a spiritual truth or God-encounter to an object, so that when the worshippers see that object outside of the sanctuary they may be reminded of that experience.

We could create these visuals by bringing in copies of paintings like the one I provided above or by projecting still life photos on a sanctuary wall to evoke an emotion or prompt a conversation. But, in the spirit of adding dimension and proximity to the illustration, I would like to suggest that you imagine the Communion table and the front of the sanctuary as your own canvas. For example, one year when Earth Day fell on a Sunday, the confirmation class and I planned and led the worship together. We were hoping to take the worshippers to the "happy places" in their lives, the spaces in nature that they associated with feeling safe and grateful. The prayers, songs, and community conversations that contributed to the worship experience were infused with images of local flora, fauna, streams, ponds, lakes, and mountains. As an invitation and inspiration to visualize the bounty for which we gave thanks, we created a flowing river out of various shades of blue fabric, punctuated it with granite rocks (from "The Granite State," where we lived), and placed lush green plants alongside the river. The nature still life reinforced the message, gave worshippers a focal point during prayers and hymns, and helped them imagine those happy places and events that connected them to the message of the day. While it would also be a great idea to hold the service outside, and we did arrange a nature walk following the worship service, the still life allowed those who would have been uncomfortable outside or who could not join the walk to enter into the spirit of the day within the sanctuary.

Symbols as the Artwork of Belief: Still Life Illustrations

Let me provide you with a couple more examples of still life experiences I have created for my congregations.

Yarn, China, and Pearls

I wrote and told three stories for my reflection during worship. The first was about an Italian grandmother who was crocheting as she sat outside her flat on the cobblestone street that hugged her family home in rural northern Italy. The second was about a college student whose mother was killed by a drunk driver, and whose aunt abided with him in his grief by inviting him to throw china at a wailing wall and, weeks later, use the pieces to create something beautiful. The third was about an oyster that had been damaged by an anchor tossed to the sea floor, setting in process the creation of a precious pearl. All the while that worshippers were listening to the stories, they could focus on a display on the table at the front of the sanctuary, just below the pulpit. A crochet hook protruded from a large basket filled with balls of yarn. The basket was surrounded by pieces of broken china, and pearls were draped throughout the tableau. The hope was that the worshippers might resonate with the experiences and symbols shared in the moment and allow them to echo into the future, reassured by the promise of the scripture of the day, 1 John 3:1–3. I reminded them that living this life we've been given, as individuals and in community, does not always follow a pattern. We aren't always mindful of when we should take our anger to the wailing wall, rather than throw things or words at inappropriate times, places, and people. We sometimes opt for meeting hurt with hurt, rather than lapping it with our greatest strength. At every turn, we must remember, "Beloved, we are God's children." Our greatest strength is Love, the God we have come from, the One Who Holds What Is Yet to Be Revealed, and the Keeper of Our Lives, when we are most faithful and when we can't do anything right.

Quilts, Bread, and Pottery

For a summer sermon series, I asked the artisans in the congregation if they would share their reflections on how the process and substance of their craft constitute a spiritual practice for them. Each week, the testifying artist would create a display from the instruments and products of his or her artistry. One Sunday the entire front of the sanctuary was ablaze with colorful quilts. Another week, on Communion Sunday, our table was heaping with artisan breads of various sizes, shapes, colors, textures, and aromas that made our mouths water. Worshippers were invited to hold and mold clay as two pottery artists created a piece of art in the center of the sanctuary, while reflecting upon God as potter as depicted in Jeremiah 18.

Guiding the Congregation's Attention using Still Life Tableaus

Creating a still life tableau is not something you would do every week. Constancy is for the spiritual objects of your tradition that your community has prayerfully and consciously decided to place in the worship space. Still life tableaus are an occasional means of adding dimension to the worship experience, helping to direct the worshippers' attention to where the worship planner wants it to be.

When you have an image or experience that is central to your reflection for the day—a metaphor or an illustration of a spiritual truth—take some time to prayerfully sit with that image or experience.

How would you describe the image?

What are the tangible objects associated with the experience?

If you were to attempt to convey the image or experience using only visuals, what would those visuals be?

Consider how you might bring that visual representation into the worship space by

- using the actual object,
- creating a symbolic representation of the image using fabric,

- projecting a picture,
- assembling a collection of objects that point to the experience you are lifting up, creating a three-dimensional collage.

Consider where you will place the tableau, with the intention of helping to guide the worshippers' attention while not overwhelming the worship experience as a whole. Is it in a place where everyone can see it? Do you need to create more than one tableau and place them in different areas so everyone can see the image?

Set up the tableau prior to worshippers, including musicians, arriving for worship. The initial impact of a striking, or even just unusual, tableau begs the worshipper to step into a journey from the first moment of curiosity.

Symbols as Windows to Seeing God

If you're a parent, you have probably heard that one of the strategies for getting your children to eat healthy foods is to invite them to help prepare the food. If they feel some ownership and pride in the preparation, they may be more willing to eat it and discover that it tastes good. Perhaps you've heard of a "pizza garden" in which many of the ingredients for creating a pizza are grown. The children plant the oregano, the basil, the tomatoes, and whatever other vegetables they might like on their pizza. They tend the garden, harvest the herbs and the vegetables, and build their pizza. Participating in the process of creating the pizza offers a multidimensional, memorable experience. So it may be with creating visuals for an engaging, emotional worship experience.

As a congregation becomes more accustomed to my use of still life displays as the artwork of belief, I begin inviting them to participate in creating the tableaus as spiritual expressions within the worship service. For example, during one Black History Month, we brought Psalm 30 to life. It was a Communion Sunday. Four members of the congregation told the stories of four black Americans who persevered through adversity and, by Grace, made a lasting contribution to society. Each reader walked up the center aisle of the sanctuary, carrying a wooden chair. The chair was placed at the Communion table before the reader approached the microphone to read the story. The stories were separated by the reading of verses from Psalm 30, extolling the power of God in lifting us from the depths. After the chairs had been placed and the stories told, we were left with a Communion table that had four empty chairs alongside it. I then shared the following message:

> As we prepare to gather at the table of Communion, where all are to be welcomed, valued, and graced in equal measure, we see four empty chairs. Even now, there are children of God being excluded from our gatherings, our workplaces, our neighborhoods, our schools, our clubs, and our churches. Even now, when many young people think that racism, sexism, and homophobia are old-fashioned, there are still oppressors on playgrounds, in corporate offices, in academia, in local and national governments, and in churches who oppose equal rights for all people of God. Districts are redrawn to minimize the impact of black voters. Mortgage lenders, academic institutions, and employers assess applications differently based on the applicant's skin color or country of origin. With every pastoral transition in my life, I am reminded that some remove my chair from the table because of my gender and because of whom I love.
>
> If all children of God are to be invited and affirmed to participate in the fullness of life that God intends, each of us is among those who must bring Psalm 30 to life. We, as individuals and as a church, are the hands and hearts, decision makers and legislators, listeners and speakers who will draw those currently excluded from the table into our communion. We are the ones who must identify the voices that are missing from the conversation and create space for them to join in and be heard. We are the ones who have the power to turn mourning into dancing, swap one's wardrobe of sackcloth for festal dress, and imagine a human community that celebrates the gifts and potential of every individual given life by God.
>
> Come to the table today, grateful that you are welcome here. It is no small gift of God's grace. All the while, consider, too, those still seeking an invitation.[4]

Another instance when the worshippers were invited to engage the still life created in the sanctuary was when we were reflecting upon walls. Once again, on the Communion table, I had built a wall out of small,

---

4. Tarolli, worship service, Congregational Church of Henniker, NH, February 4, 2018.

one-inch-square wooden blocks that I purchased at a craft store. It was a curved wall that serpentined across the table. At the beginning of my reflection, I invited those gathered to focus on the wall as I offered brief, interesting factoids about significant human-made walls across generations and the globe. I reminded them that there are walls that are visible human constructs that you can see and touch. And there are walls that are invisible human constructs but seemingly as impermeable as cement blocks or forged steel. There are walls, visible and invisible, that are protective and healthy. And there are walls that are protective and unhealthy.

We then had a congregational conversation during which they were asked to share what they would identify as some protective and healthy walls, walls that serve or promote a common good, and what they would identify as some unhealthy walls, walls that undermine the pursuit of a common good. We considered how Jesus calls us to dismantle barriers (Eph 2:11–22). At the end of the reflection, I invited the worshippers to take a moment to consider the visible and invisible walls that existed in their own lives and the walls they identified in the place and practice of their church. In the words of Robert Frost, I asked them to consider what they were "walling in or walling out,"[5] with or without intention. They were encouraged to identify at least one change they could make that would help to break down a wall that no longer serves a common good. In the moments that followed, they were welcome to approach the Communion table, take a piece of the wall that was erected there, helping to dismantle it, and offer a prayer that they would be given the honesty, strength, and creativity to do the same with the walls in their lives. They were invited to take their piece of the wall home with them as a reminder of the invitation to imagine the world without the borders that undermine the unity of which Jesus spoke.

While music has the power to elicit spontaneous, undeliberated, emotional responses, and is, therefore, a key aspect of creating the space for a visceral, transformative God-encounter in the context of worship, the use of visual images or objects is another way to invite an emotional experience without alienating or intimidating those who approach worship as a more rational or intellectual engagement of their belief and practice. Encouraging worshippers to thoughtfully and prayerfully consider a still life tableau or to participate in the shaping of that tableau in the course of worship may usher the participants to real or imagined emotional experiences in which

---

5. Frost, "Mending Wall," https://www.poetryfoundation.org/poems/44266/mending-wall.

they may discover God or Jesus or Spirit. I have heard from many parishioners who have *felt* their way into epiphanies as a result of visual stimuli.

Rituals

Breaking bread with one another as we celebrate the Lord's Supper, using water as the visible sign of being washed in a baptismal grace, lighting prayer candles in a Roman Catholic cathedral, receiving the weekly offering, or approaching the chancel rail to profess Jesus as Lord and Savior are some of the rituals that have shaped the Christian tradition for centuries. They involve, in part, the use of objects and physical movement to symbolize an inward spiritual grace. I will reflect upon some of the specific rituals we use as markers in the Christian liturgical year in the next chapter, but here we will consider how spiritual exercises done in community, involving shared objects and movements, can create experiences that engender a depth of connection among participants and with God, even as worshippers engage the ritual individually.

Here's a fun question to help illustrate my point. What do yawning, a baby's uncontrollable laughter, and the volume or tone of conversational partners have in common? Take a moment to think about it. Any thoughts? They are almost always contagious. If you are not intentionally working against your natural physiological response, you will often yawn when watching another person yawn. You will find yourself beginning to laugh when listening to the joyful giggling of an infant, and you will typically reflect the volume and tone of the one with whom you are sharing a conversation.

One mark and gift of being church is that the emotional responses and expressions of God-encounters can be contagious. The melancholy response to the lingering darkness of Jesus' crucifixion or the joy that bursts from singing a hymn of resurrection praise can crack open hearts in succession much like falling dominoes. As humans do, we then gravitate toward like-minded (or like-behaving) people. Soon a critical mass of those who share a religious experience or expression builds into a community of faith that moves and grows together.

I have been known to invite worshippers to sing and dance the Hokey Pokey as we are called to worship, because when we find ourselves singing or moving in a shared rhythm, we add to what we have in common. We are no longer individuals sitting in our usual pews, greeting those who usually sit around us, and repeating our usual habits before worship—reading the

Attending to the Language of Worship: Symbols and Ritual

inserts in the bulletin, writing our offering check, checking out the hymns. Instead, we are fully engaged in a communal event that may stretch us out of our comfort zone, but that forces us to truly see those around us and engage with them in a shared experience.

Engaging in rituals with shared objects or movements holds great potential to foster a sense of community among the worshippers through repetitive engagement, common experience, and communal reflection. It is in the midst of community that members have the opportunity to experience particular gifts of God—affirmation, belonging, lovingkindness, partnership in mission and ministry, forgiveness, generosity, and revelation.

Symbols as Windows to Seeing God: Illustrations

Particularly during the seasons of Advent and Lent, when we spend weeks journeying toward the culminating experience of Jesus' birth or resurrection, I will design a ritual that visually represents the progression and culmination of that story. Here are a couple of examples.

ACTS OF LOVE PAPER CHAIN

I created a special Advent calendar and made it available to worshippers before and during Advent. Each day named an activity that illustrated the active waiting for God's surprising breakthrough of Love, ways in which we can prepare the way for another to experience God's Love. Activities for the first two weeks of Advent included the following:

Week 1: Using the Internet, phone book, or newspaper, discover organizations that distribute clothing to those in need.

> Choose one article of clothing to donate.
> Purchase or make a winter hat, scarf, mittens, or gloves to donate.
> Pray for those who do not have enough appropriate clothing for themselves or their family.
> Tell a friend or relative about what you are doing and invite them to join you.
> Deliver your offerings to one of the organizations you identified.

Week 2: Using the Internet, phone book, or newspaper, discover organizations that provide food to those in need in your town.

> Choose your favorite non-perishable meal item and your favorite non-perishable dessert to donate.
> Read one article (newspaper, magazine, Internet) to learn more about the issue of hunger.
> Pray for those who do not have enough nutritious food or drink for themselves or their family.
> Tell a friend or relative about what you are doing and invite them to join you.
> Deliver your offerings to one of the organizations you identified.

During each Sunday worship, participants were invited to write on a one-by-four-inch piece of construction paper one activity they did that prepared the way for another to experience God's Love. They then carried their paper to the front of the sanctuary and added it to the paper chain that lay on the Communion table, growing each week. On Christmas Eve, the chain was hung on a tree in the sanctuary, which was then lit as we celebrated the Light of Christ coming into the world.

Prayer Ribbons and Praise Blossoms

You may be familiar with the flower cross ritual that has become an Easter tradition in some churches. I believe it's important to engage the worshipper in the journey through the wilderness of Lent, so that the Easter joy may be more palpable in the worship experience. Toward that end, occasionally I have adapted the flower ritual to include the journey to the cross on a weekly basis.

For example, one year I offered a series of reflections on the wilderness experiences defined by some of the "seven deadly sins." Following from the sermon or reflection of the day, during which the worshippers had the opportunity to consider how a particular sin, say pride, had shaped them and their behaviors for better or for worse, the worshippers would be invited to carry those thoughts to a large wooden cross standing at the front of the sanctuary, take a strip of purple fabric from a nearby basket, and tie it onto the chicken wire wrapped around the cross, offering a silent prayer. It was a gesture to recalibrate with the Holy. It was a sign and symbol of some prideful part of oneself or one's community that might be given over to God, given up, allowed to die, creating in them or their wider community space for new life. Over time, the cross filled with prayer ribbons of various shades of purple. People were moved to see the growing representation of the prayers of their community. On Easter morning, the cross was turned around, there were a few flowers tucked in the chicken wire that covered the cross, and baskets of cut flowers were placed nearby. After the resurrection reflection, worshippers were invited to come forward and say a prayer of thanksgiving for an instance of resurrection being made manifest in their lives or the lives of those they cared about, and to place a flower in the chicken wire. The colorful, beautiful cross was transformed into a visual testimony to the resurrected Christ. What was even more striking was that some of the ends of purple cloth were still visible around the flowers as a symbol of answered prayer.

Guiding the Congregation's Attention by Incorporating Original Ritual

When introducing a new ritual in the worship experience, it is beneficial to plan on using it several weeks in a row, so that worshippers can enter into it as the Spirit moves them. Some may be more comfortable watching one week and engaging more fully another week. Don't underestimate the power of observation to move people as well. It can be a blessing to watch a group of individuals approach the focal point of the ritual and prayerfully participate. One might gratefully say, "If today I do not have the faith to move, I am heartened by those who do."

For that reason, and because I like to emphasize the *journey* of Advent and Lent toward birth and resurrection, those seasons are conducive to a ritual like those described above and in the next chapter. I have occasionally created a ritual to accompany a sermon series at some other time of year as well.

Choose a season or series during which you would like to invite the worshippers into a deeper, transformative spiritual experience using ritual. Consider images that resonate with the season or series you have chosen. For example, I once created a dark wilderness out of black construction paper on a black background. The ritual involved placing white dots on the board in such a way that, over time, the points of light gave definition, clarity, and increasing brightness in the wilderness.

How might you use fabric, natural elements, candles, paper, or other simple objects to engage the worshipper in an act of devotion? You will find more examples in the next chapter.

Keep in Mind

The images don't have to be literal. The important thing is that the focal point of the ritual grows from week to week, illustrating progress in the journey toward culmination.

Consider how the focal point will change to represent that culminating moment in the season or series.

The ritual act should be accessible to all, not too complicated to navigate with mind or body. You don't want to disturb the prayerful and emotional moment by introducing a set of instructions that requires excessive cognitive deliberation.

For those who may not be comfortable approaching the ritual space during the worship service, invite them to participate before or after the worship service, as the Spirit moves them.

While worship planners may create still life tableaus and interactive rituals to help guide the worshippers into a moving encounter with God or a change of heart that holds an epiphany, these shared rituals also create the

Attending to the Language of Worship: Symbols and Ritual

opportunity for a shared emotional experience in and of themselves. Adults help children connect their link in the chain or tie their strip of fabric to the cross. Couples perform the ritual together in a joint prayer. Younger, more nimble fingers guide arthritic hands in tying a knot. And everyone joins in actively building a visual focal point that becomes a compass—anchor and guide—for their journey through the season.

5

Attending to the Story

It was never about the pizza. We gathered. Crossing town and circling up in the living room were two schoolteachers, a secretary, an auto parts salesman, a housewife, an Italian immigrant who sewed leather handbags and crocheted wedding afghans, a child who loved to read, a child who loved sports, and a child who loved Love. Three generations were we. A small pile of brightly wrapped gifts grew in the corner of the room. A decorated, homemade cake graced the center of the dining table. Not long after we settled into conversation, with the accompaniments of drinks and snacks, she phoned in the pizza order. Chatter filled the room. There were fishing stories, school stories from the perspectives of the teachers and the students, stories about local townspeople, and stories about the relatives "across the pond." There were check-ins on check-ups and sports chatter by self-appointed armchair analysts. We learned, we remembered, we laughed, we gossiped, we debated, we researched, we planned, we cared, we congratulated—and we ate pizza. The guest of honor blew out candles and opened gifts. We ate cake and ice cream and, soon thereafter, we each retreated to the places we called home.

This is how my family celebrated birthdays throughout my childhood. Every time we celebrated, we ate pizza, but it was never about the pizza. It was about gathering together, telling stories, and marking time.

Attending to the Story

The Liturgical Calendar: Gathering Together, Telling Stories, and Marking Time

The Christian liturgical calendar, born from the communal beliefs and practices of the early church, is also an invitation to Christian brothers and sisters to gather together, tell stories, and mark time. After the death and resurrection of Jesus, before the Gospels were written and the councils drafted creeds as the unifying instruments of Christian belief, those faithful to the truths Jesus lived and taught came together in person and in real time to remember him. Coming together for prayer on the Lord's Day was an extension of the Jewish communal practices that shaped the lives of the earliest Christian believers. Weekly vigils testified to their hope, as these apocalyptic believers prayed for the imminent return of Jesus, bringing God's kingdom to fulfillment. Memories of the life, ministry, death, and resurrection of Jesus were the buoys keeping them afloat in their waiting.

Over the course of the first four centuries of the Common Era, gatherings, stories, and ritual markers of time began to shape the weekly and yearly rhythms of Jesus' followers in the form of annual feasts and seasons of preparation. At the worship table, bread was broken and wine was poured in the memory and hope of God's reach into the world through Jesus, the anointed and risen one.

While specific dates and traditions for Easter, Holy Week, and the season of Lent would shift with the tides of Christian communities in different cultural contexts, the anchors of the Christian liturgical calendar would always be the passion and resurrection of Jesus. Early followers of Jesus, separated by space and time from the earthly life of their Messiah, did not have access to information about him beyond the spoken and sparsely written testimonies bequeathed to them. Nonetheless, much like adoring parents overstuffing scrapbooks as they chronicle the life of their first child, those indebted to Jesus' saving grace wanted to capture every significant moment of his life, even if it required a little imagination to fill in the blanks. Compelled by belief, they gathered, they told stories, and they marked time on a daily, weekly, monthly, and yearly schedule.

Even now, almost two millennia later, there has not been a great deal of revision to the liturgical calendar of the early Christian tradition. The length of the seasons of preparation, Lent and Advent, has fluctuated. The timing of Easter and Christmas is not constant throughout Christendom. Pentecost was once a season and is now a day. Early American Protestantism pared down liturgies to such an extent that many of the markers on the Christian liturgical calendar were left on the cutting room floor. In some Christian traditions, the "special Sundays" on the calendar are more often associated with causes of social justice or institutional advancement rather than the story that shapes our essential Christian hope and discipleship.

The loss of attentiveness to the Christian liturgical calendar as a continual annual reel of the story shared between the Divine and the human, then and now, robs us of a significant invitation to gather together, tell stories, and mark time as seekers and believers in the twenty-first century. Yet, it is in the gathering, the storytelling, and the marking of time that we care for one another, discover our identity, learn from our past, and imagine our future as the beloved community.

Biblical Story as Compass

Paying Attention to Your Story in the Biblical Story

Situate yourself in a space and position conducive to quiet reflection. Take a few slow, deep, cleansing breaths. Identify a hurt, a care, or a concern that you are carrying in your heart today. How does it make you feel? What are you praying for relative to your hurt, care, or concern? Hold your circumstances, your feelings, and your needs up to the light of God's grace. Without being concerned about identifying chapter and verse, consider a Bible story that resonates with your situation. Take time to sift through all the stories that come to mind before you settle on one. Find that story in the Bible. Read it through slowly a few times. How does it resonate with your story? What guidance, comfort, or hope does the story offer?

If one goal of worship planning is to usher the attention of the worshippers into an emotional, transformative spiritual encounter with God, then the Jesus story is the compass for setting the direction of worship planners and leaders. While emotional experiences are essential, they cannot be the end game for the Christian worship experience. Ultimately, we must give those emotional experiences—the changes of heart, the aha-moments, the God-encounters—meaning in the context of a larger story. If we are to cultivate Christian faith and build the beloved community, we must see ourselves as both participants in the story as well as stewards of the story. We can dive into the experience of God, wallow in the blessings, wrestle with doubt, taste redemption, and glimpse heaven, but it only nurtures a community of faith when we gather together and find our place in the midst of a shared story.

Jesus tells us to proclaim the good news (Mark 16:15) and to be his witnesses (Acts 1:8). That is only possible if the faithful *choose* the good news story to be the rubric that informs and is reflected in their own lives. Valuing the Jesus story as a guide to life may seem obvious to faithful churchgoers, but one of the struggles of contemporary churches is that the twenty-first century gives people many options to choose from when they look for a story that might offer meaning and purpose to their existence. Members of Alcoholics Anonymous may use the story of Dr. Bob and Bill W., whose rubric is the twelve steps to recovery. Cinephiles use the plotlines of movies as the defining illustrations of where they fit in the context of the universe. Confessions of faith go viral in the form of tweets and digital pictures when terrorists attack the heart of the United States. This cyber-gospel is not lifted from the Christian story necessarily, but rather it is written by the poets, musicians, and brokenhearted and hope-filled people of the day. And so, thirsty spiritual pilgrims who are feeling grief, fear, anger, joy, sadness, or loneliness slip away from the sanctuaries of churches and find community and a relevant, accessible story in AA meetings and virtual chatrooms. The fullness of being church in the world erodes because we fail to meet the living in the depths of their beings where they *feel* the circumstances, needs, and celebrations of life. The present and future vitality of Christian worship and community is dependent upon our making meaningful connections between the Jesus story and our own and helping others to do the same. In so doing, we will extend the story of our faith and proclaim the Good News through age-old stories, as well as new experiences and personal testimonies of twenty-first-century Advents, Epiphanies, Good Fridays, and Easter resurrections.

Reclaiming Ritual

We may light the Advent wreath, cast and costume the Christmas pageant, flip flapjacks on "Fat Tuesday," and don ashes on Ash Wednesday. We may look for baby Jesus in the kings' cake on Epiphany, worship at sunrise on Easter, wear red on the day of Pentecost, and light candles on All Saints' Day. When we talk about the liturgical calendar of the Christian tradition, annual rituals are often the tags that identify the seasons. Local congregations develop their own "pizza parties" to gather together, tell stories, and mark time, but, unlike my family's birthday celebrations, it often becomes all about the pizza.

The rituals couched in the various liturgical seasons often lure the attention of the participants *away from* the experience or truth they were intended to affirm rather than *deeper into* the meaning and relevance of the story. The ritual often *replaces* the chapter of the Christian story that defines the season rather than inviting participants to *experience* the story. To-do lists, production values, volunteer recruitment, shopping, and building and polishing the icon of an annual tradition hold the story prisoner.

In time, the sentimental preservation of local traditions erodes the community's visceral connection to the story. People depart from the sanctuary talking about how *that* version of the ritual measured up to years past, rather than feeling or experiencing the gospel anew in their midst. In addition, we lose the opportunity to discover a new emotional resonance with the story, open ourselves to deeper communion with God, and tell the story in our own words, expanding the language of our faith for a new generation of believers. One local church recited the same Advent wreath candle-lighting liturgy for eighteen years. Another maintained the tradition of creating a crèche out of two-liter soda bottles for more than two decades. In many Protestant churches, the ministry of the board of deacons, or a similar group, has been reduced to orchestrating the logistics around such long-held rituals, season to season. If they are efficient, they have a two-inch three-ring binder filled with how-to instructions, passed from generation to generation. But when was the last time the members of these congregations talked about, reflected upon, and even wrestled with the piece of the Christian story that such traditions were intended to represent?

While there is room for the respectful and reverent keeping of some traditions, a fruitful balance of tradition and innovation in liturgies will welcome the Spirit to dance in new ways through the worship experience. Traditions may be joyfully or routinely embraced for their sentimental familiarity, their generational continuity, or because they genuinely move people year after year. At the same time, those habitual markers of time in Christian communities may also ring hollow because the essential gospel has ceased to be at the center. What purpose does creating a creche out of any materials or pulling the old wooden or ceramic one out of storage once a year serve if those attending the Christmas Eve service do not feel the significance of the birth of the baby who lies in the cattle trough in the stable and do not embrace the idea that even the least among us have the potential to change the world? There comes a time when worship planners and leaders would best serve the worshipping community by playing in the sandbox of spiritual reflection, discovering anew their stories in the Jesus story and vice versa.

Reimagining the Advent Experience

The season is Advent. It is a season of preparation that grew, in part, as a mirror reflection of the season of preparation that is Lent. As communities of believers wanted to mark time with the occasion of Jesus' birth—the earthly beginning of the resurrected one's life—the feast day of Christmas was established and a season of preparation was shaped by days of fasting and scripture readings.[1] Christian churches have been shaping their Advent rituals around whichever theology has informed their understanding since the sixth century: remembering the historical birth of Jesus, considering how the birth of Jesus can be personally or communally transforming in the present, or anticipating the return of the risen Christ as harbinger of the fulfillment of God's intention for the created universe. The language for liturgy is informed by what we believe about whose coming we are anticipating, the preparation required, and the consequences for which we hope.

Time and time again, we have biblical affirmation that one story can be told truthfully, even if differently, from multiple perspectives. The two different perspectives on the birth narrative in the Gospels of Matthew and Luke exemplify that stories are often told through the lens of what the storyteller deems significant, either to the storyteller or to the audience. If

---

1. While the word "advent" is derived from the Latin word meaning "to come," liturgy scholar Martin J. Connell suggests that this *one* word has led to multiple interpretations of the season's meaning. In "The Origins and Evolution of Advent in the West," he identifies three different traditions that have defined Advent. The one tradition is primarily *scriptural*, with its theology and rhetoric based on the infancy narratives of the New Testament. Another tradition is fundamentally *ascetic*, with its contexts usually domestic or monastic. The third tradition is the *eschatological*, based theologically on the notion that the *adventus* to which Christian communities would be attentive is the coming of Christ at the end of time rather than the *fait accompli* in the manger at Bethlehem (351).

there is a variety of experience and expression in the very Gospel stories that give meaning to our Advent season of waiting, then surely our twenty-first-century rituals can display the same richness. When you begin to pray your way into a new ritual expression, don't get hung up on there being a right way and a wrong way to design the ritual. If the purpose of the ritual is to welcome engagement in the story that is unfolding—gather, tell stories, and mark time—then there is no right and wrong. There is accessible and inaccessible. There is meaningful and meaningless. There is relevant and irrelevant. Here are some rituals that have proven to be meaningful during Advent in communities where I have served.

> ### *Guiding the Congregation's Attention to Reimagining the Advent Wreath Candle-Lighting Ritual*
>
> Many Western Christian churches will include the lighting of the Advent wreath in their weekly worship liturgy throughout the season of Advent. The candle-lighting liturgy provides an opportunity to employ our own contemporary and experiential language in celebrating the growing Light as we anticipate God's breakthrough. Here are some invitations that are variations on old themes:
>
> - Explore the candle-lighting liturgies of different cultures, allowing the liturgy of a distant land, a partner church, or a different denomination to bless the Advent journey.
> - Consider the genealogy in the Gospel of Matthew (1:1–17). Name each of the four candles after four different individuals in that litany of names, describing the thread they carry in the gospel story.
> - Have the congregation sing one verse of the hymn "People, Look East" (Farjeon/Shaw) as an introit or call to worship, then create a liturgy that uses Guest, Rose, Star, and Lord as the focus for each candle on the Advent wreath, mirroring the final line of each of the four verses.
> - Identify four words that describe how the humans in the Jesus story felt as they anticipated his birth. Acknowledge

Attending to the Story

> their stories and how those human emotions that we all experience help or hinder us in opening ourselves to Emmanuel (God with us).
>
> - With the lighting of each candle, share the story of a current situation that is in need of experiencing God's reach into the world that we celebrate with Jesus' birth.
>
> - Use a traditional set of words for the candles—e.g., hope, peace, joy, and love—and write original prose or poetry for each week's candle-lighting liturgy, embracing both tradition and the context of the gathered community (see Appendix 4).

In some Christian worship traditions, there is still a very distinct line between the priest and the people. The chancel and the altar are spaces reserved for worship leaders while the worshippers take their places in the pews. One way to encourage worshippers to explore and express their faith in their own words and life experiences is by welcoming their participation in the sacred spaces of the sanctuary into which they may not have previously had access, especially during the worship service. In the previous chapter, I suggested that the invitation for parishioners to leave their pews, come forward, and take some sort of action in a ritual provides the opportunity to physically embody the prayers of the moment. When this action is taken in or around the chancel area of the sanctuary, the worshippers' presence and their individual stories are affirmed as part of God's story. Their wisdom and their prayers are as significant as anyone else's. Ritual is not reserved for those wearing stoles or those selected to fill the coveted roles of candle lighters, Communion servers, or offertory gift bearers. Ritual informed by the stories we are living in the present can be just as meaningful as ritual shaped by the spiritual pilgrims of the early church.

Moving beyond the Lighting of the Advent Wreath

Especially because cyclical celebrations couched in the liturgical seasons can become habitual or rote or laden with local traditions that have lost a dynamic connection to the story they represent, inviting worshippers to participate in a ritual that is different from year to year encourages them to consider the gospel story anew, perhaps through a different lens. The ritual may be one that grows visually week to week, paralleling the increasing light of the Advent wreath. This conveys continuity and community in the journey through the season. Here are some ideas:

- Place a manger (a rustic trough made of wood with straw that would feed the animals in the stable) in a prominent, accessible space at the front of the sanctuary. Next to the manger, place a basket filled with strips of white cloth. Invite worshippers to bring into their hearts and minds a person, situation, or place that needs the birth of God's Holy Surprise. They may select a thirsty place in their own lives, in the life of someone they care about, or in a distant land. Invite them to carry that thought with them as they come forward to the manger. As they place a piece of "swaddling cloth" (Luke 2:12) in the manger, they are invited to offer a related silent or spoken prayer.

- The same invitation to prayer can be extended using a different activity: hanging a star anise on a garland of fir pine that graces the chancel rail; pinning colored pushpins on a map of the world identifying the location of the person or situation for which prayer is needed; weaving pieces of colored paper, ribbon, or fabric into a grapevine wreath.

- Each week of Advent a piece of tissue paper is placed at the end of each pew. Week 1 is dark purple, week 2 is lavender, week 3 is aqua, and week 4 is pale blue. The worshippers are invited to tear a piece of the tissue paper off, carry it forward, and place it in a tall, clear, glass cylinder as they offer their prayers. As the Advent season unfolds, the papers accumulate and lighten with anticipation of the coming of the Light of the World. On Christmas Eve, the glass cylinder has been transformed. The tissue has been applied (shellacked) to the outside of the cylinder and, accompanied by words of prayer for wholeness on the eve of Emmanuel, a candle is lit inside the cylinder, shining through the four weeks of prayers.

Remembering the importance of music in creating or intensifying an emotional experience, as the worshippers participate in the ritual, the church musician might offer instrumental "walking music" that sets the emotional tone. The choice for music is not necessarily based on the lyrics of a song or hymn. It should not be a sung piece that worshippers are listening to for a message; rather it should reflect the mood of the experience.

Attending to the Story

The music should not be the focus of the ritual. It should be one way of moving the worshippers to participate because the self-consciousness they might feel has given way to immersion in the emotion of the moment.

Inhabiting the Bible Story

Throughout the previous chapters, we have been attending to the language of worship as it is constituted by words, music, objects, and ritual. As worship planners and leaders, one of our goals is to invite worshippers into an emotionally engaging experience in which they may recognize the movement of the Divine and transformation in their own hearts. Designing such a worship experience requires spiritual reflection, as well as using the breadth of expression available to us.

You might begin by considering how the community in which you currently plan or lead worship marks the various seasons on the liturgical calendar. Treading lightly, with gentleness and reverence, choose one worship experience from one liturgical season that you would like to revise or revive because it has become stale, is not emotionally engaging, or is focused too much on the pizza and not on experiencing God through the biblical story. Ask yourself (or those responsible for worship planning with you), "What are we attending to in this worship experience?" "What do we wish we were attending to?" The exercise below might help you answer these questions.

> *Guiding the Congregation's Attention through*
> *Expanding the Language of Worship*
>
> To refresh the worship experience that you have identified and create the emotional and spiritual space for a God-encounter, identify a Bible story that relates to that worship experience. Spend some time reflecting upon the story, making notes as you go.
>
> > What is the context of the story?
> > What is happening?
> > Who are the characters?
> > What might each one be feeling as the story unfolds? Why?

Then, immerse yourself in the story through empathizing with the characters, their setting, and their situation. For example, if you wanted to revise or revive the worship experience that is based upon the annunciation and foretelling of Jesus' birth, begin by reading Luke 1:26–38, and consider the following questions, making notes as you go.

> Who is Mary? Who is Gabriel? Who is Elizabeth?
> Where do you imagine this scene taking place? Where is Mary? What might she have been doing before Gabriel arrived? Why is she alone?
> How might Gabriel be feeling as he approaches Mary? Why? Would he be concerned about her?
> What might be Gabriel's demeanor toward Mary?
> How might Mary be feeling when she encounters Gabriel and then when she hears his news?
> What might be Mary's demeanor in her initial response to Gabriel's news? Why?
> What might Mary's feelings and demeanor be as the angel departs?
> How might you feel if you were in the role of Mary? Gabriel?

Once you have refreshed your own understanding and experience of the story, imagine different ways you might tell the story:

> A dramatic reading or performance of the story (using only the characters' voices, movements, and expressions)
> Music capturing the emotions of Gabriel and Mary (using improvised or conventional musical instruments; singing; recorded music)
> Gestures/movement/dance capturing the emotions of the scene
> Storytelling (using a personal or published story that is a parallel illustration of the biblical story)
> Inviting people to recall (and perhaps share) a moment when they were Gabriel and had to give some momentous and unexpected news to someone or when they were Mary and heard such news

What are the words or stories, music, objects, or movements that have risen to the top as you have moved through this reflection? How might you incorporate one or more of

> those as a focal point in the worship service to invite listeners into an emotional, empathic experience of the story, with the hope of creating the space for a transformative spiritual experience or change of heart?

Becoming the Storytellers of Holy Week

When the worshipping community has been invited to testify in their own words about God's activity in their lives by way of worship rituals or spiritual practices and reflection, they can enter the Jesus story in a more meaningful way. Joan Chittister describes the liturgical year as follows:

> It takes us from one growth point of soul to the next until we come to understand the meaning of the moment, until we come to realize that the life of Jesus is the template of our own. If we are really meant to follow Jesus, then we must follow Jesus into every dimension of life, including into the suffering that is the price of it. We must look closely at how He handles each moment of life, what He expects in every situation, whom He helps, whom He chides, what He holds out as the ideal. Indeed, the life of Jesus is not a monument to the past; it is an invitation to the fullness of our own futures.[2]

The piece of the story that is the defining narrative of the Christian tradition unfolds during the days of Holy Week on the liturgical calendar. As with most dates and seasons in the Christian tradition, communities have marked the time of Jesus' passion and resurrection differently over the course of the centuries. For some, the focus is on the resurrection. For others, the focus is on the suffering. Sometimes, the remembrance is contained within one long service of worship. Other times, the chapters of Jesus' last days are played out in a rhythm that resonates with the biblical story: his entry into Jerusalem (Palm Sunday); his ministry in and around the temple (Monday through Wednesday); his intimate gathering with disciples for a shared meal and foot washing, interrupted by betrayal and arrest (Maundy Thursday); his crucifixion (Good Friday); the vigil of grief and anticipation (Saturday); and the resurrection (Sunday). Some will fast. Some will prepare for baptism. Some will carry the cross, and others will don bonnets. There are passion plays,

---

2. Chittister, *Liturgical Year*, 124.

foot washings, the seven last words, and Easter egg hunts. Flowers color the sanctuary; resurrection is heralded with favorite hymns; and "Christ is risen! He is risen indeed!" resonates in languages and lands worldwide. When the most significant week on the liturgical calendar is layered with centuries of traditions, how do we make the story our own in the twenty-first century? Is there even room or permission to tell the story in our own language, broadly defined, building upon the cherished lexicon of our faith?

Testimony

While I was serving a church in the Vermont Conference of the United Church of Christ, the conference board of directors invited all the local congregations in the conference to reflect upon "faith at the edges . . ." Groups could complete the sentence however the Spirit moved them: faith at the edges of power, faith at the edges of sobriety, faith at the edges of sustainability, faith at the edges of the unknown, or faith at the edges of doubt, to name a few possibilities.

In previous years, Palm/Passion Sunday services in which I had been involved often included testimony put in the mouths of those imagined to be present at the procession and the events that followed, a form of midrash. We read scripture. We identified the characters in the stories, and we imagined what they might have felt, thought, or said as they witnessed Jesus' last days. During the year of considering "faith at the edges," I invited members of the congregation to imagine *themselves* at the edges of the events that took place in those precious moments. Having nurtured a culture of sharing our faith questions, our Spirit-sightings, and our wrestling matches with God, this was another invitation to testify by putting ourselves in the familiar story of Jesus. The exercise was moving and worshipful for those who spoke and those who listened as these perspectives on the story were interspersed with biblical versions during worship (see Appendix 5).

One way to elicit these kinds of profound testimonies is simply to ask for them. However, there is the risk that the question will overwhelm someone. It is not unlike when someone is asked a question such as "What did you like the *most* about the movie?" or "What is the *hardest* thing you've ever done?" Those questions might stump someone as they worry about the added step of prioritizing their experiences. Instead, "What did you like about the movie?" or "Tell me about something in your life that has challenged you" are often more accessible questions. So it is with testifying about faith beliefs and experiences. Just the word "testify" can shut some people down. Instead, imagining themselves in the story provides an entry point for conversation.

Sensory Experience

If ritual, spiritual practice, and theological reflection have not been part of someone's experience, then putting words to their questions and beliefs may be elusive. Talking about the difficult or confusing events of Jesus' last days—his rebellion at the temple, betrayal, conviction, crucifixion, and bodily resurrection—can be challenging for leaders and followers alike, especially as pastors and congregational leaders attempt to sustain an inclusive church community in places where religious affiliation is diminishing. However, the apologetic avoidance or revision of the story creates a distance from the narrative that threatens to erode the very foundation of our faith: a belief in God's promise of a liberating hope. Instead of figuring out how to *explain* the story in a new way, we can attempt to *tell* the story in a new way.

Consider how the worshippers might see, hear, taste, smell, or touch the story. Objects, color, sound, artwork, symbols, and sacrament can tell the story: palms, candles, bread, wine or juice, crowds jeering and cheering, the chains of arrest, a crown of thorns, a cross being dragged, a hammer pounding nails into a piece of wood, white cloths. While reading the biblical story, we can also illustrate it, appealing to the senses as if we were there.

When separate services take place on each day in Holy Week, visual representations in the sanctuary provide continuity between the chapters of the story. For example, palms left scattered and drying out in the sanctuary and on the Communion table at the end of the Palm/Passion Sunday service become part of the tableau for the Maundy Thursday service. The Communion table is in the condition it was left in after the Maundy Thursday service—remnants of elements and extinguished candles—so that worshippers connect that piece of the story with the Good Friday or Easter Vigil chapter, whichever is next for the congregation.

The very events that gave life to the Christian faith and tradition may be on the verge of becoming the least relevant, and that irrelevance is perhaps the most corrosive element for the present and future church. Passion plays, the veneration of the cross, and Easter vigils are increasingly esoteric, habitual rituals for confirmed believers rather than profoundly moving faith experiences holding revelation and hope for believers and seekers alike. It is perhaps more challenging, but nonetheless important, for Christian communities to be prayerfully creative in sharing the story that unfolds during Holy Week. The traditional words and rituals that took shape in the early centuries of the Common Era may not always resonate as invitation, proclamation, or liberation, though they ought not to be dispensed with out of hand. A faithful balance of tradition and innovation in storytelling and ritual is necessary if we are going to welcome one and all into the fullness of God's activity of redemption and resurrection.

A Living Proclamation

It's not about the pizza. It is about gathering together, telling stories, and marking time—bequeathing and building a community of Christian faith. In many twenty-first-century churches, people do not want to be told *what* to believe, nor do they want to talk *about* religion. Belief comes from experiencing God in real time. The Christian liturgical year gives us the rhythms and story for creating transformative spiritual experiences, God-encounters, which lead to a more relevant and vital faith life, personally and communally.

As many traditional church communities become threadbare, the strands of storytelling that testify to a living God begin to unravel. The Bible, worship, and testimonies that have long informed and inspired pilgrims on the Way are overlooked without intention and, in time, are deemed superfluous. The tapestry woven from generations of sacred stories that tell of healing, recovery, abandonment, rescue, renewal, forgiveness, and the promise and experience of new life lies dormant on the loom. It's time for us to take up the threads again and give new life to the old stories by making them a vibrant part of the worship experience. We need to *experience* each story as for the first time and *feel* its resonance in our lives, individually and as community—gathering in our sanctuaries, telling our biblical and personal stories, and celebrating those significant markers in our shared calendar.

6

Attending to the Emotional Flow of Worship

> *Paying Attention to Your Rhythms*
>
> Draw a horizontal line.
> Under the line, write the hours of one day from left to right, beginning with the time you typically wake up at the left end.
> Above the line, graph the flow of your energy level throughout the day and evening hours.
> Consider your typical daily activities relative to the flow of your energy. How does your energy level dictate the timing of your activities? How might the effectiveness or enjoyment of your activities be impacted by the corresponding level of energy? Are there changes you might make to better correlate your energy and your activities?

SOMETIMES ON A SUNDAY afternoon, after a full morning with worship and church folk, I will lie down on the couch and channel surf for the sports of the day. I don't really want to *watch* anything, but I know that the tone of the commentators at a baseball game or a golf tournament will provide the perfect sedative for a much-needed nap. As long as I'm not invested in the outcome of the competition, I can detach emotionally from the substance of the event and let the drone of the commentary carry me into sleep. There is nothing that is demanding my attention, and whatever energy remains from the morning will drain off as my body, mind, and spirit become less engaged in the world around me.

Then there are the natural rhythms of my day and my week. I am a morning person. Unless pressed by a deadline, I am not especially creative or productive in the evening. I have learned that if I don't exercise first thing in the morning, I may not exercise at all. However, I also know that if I get mired in a dilemma, a thirty-minute walk clears the cobwebs and opens the space for fresh ideas. I generally like to reach out to others in the middle of the day, and I require some time to wind down after a late-night meeting or a chorus rehearsal if I'm going to have a good night of sleep. Date night on Friday night and Saturday breakfast at one of my favorite diners are a cherished and necessary counterbalance to my work week. Monday is my sabbath. Tuesday morning, I make lists. Friday is for worship prep. These decisions about what to do when are all about the stewardship of my energy and paying attention to my natural rhythms.

Syncing Liturgical Elements with the Emotional Flow of Worship

Just as in our daily lives, the worship experience is susceptible to dips and bursts of energy that fuel or fritter the worshippers' attention. If, as worship planners and leaders, we are not conscientious in prayerfully planning worship, the give and take in the world of the sanctuary will grow stale, and there will be nothing that jars rote engagement into visceral connection with the Holy. Thinking minds will not give way to the emotional experience that is so often the seed bed of feeling or experiencing God. A transformative spiritual experience or change of heart will be elusive if we don't consider how the rhythms of worship can be shaped to provide multiple opportunities for emotional engagement.

In order to guide the worshippers' attention to where the worship leader would like it to go, the worship service must be designed as if the words, music, silence, movement, symbols, and ritual are the means by which the worshippers will travel to the intended destination. The destination is not necessarily a prescribed understanding, but rather an openness to an experience of or with God.

Attending to the Emotional Flow of Worship

> *Paying Attention to your Worship Experience . . .*
>
> ✏ Recall the last time you were especially moved during a typical Sunday worship experience, a time when you left the sanctuary feeling as though you had a unique encounter with the Divine.
>
> What was happening? How did words, music, objects, or ritual play a role in that experience? How did you feel? How did you then interpret it as a God-encounter or an aha-moment in your journey of faith? That is, what is the story or testimony you could now tell about that experience?

In previous chapters, I have suggested ways in which words, music, objects, and rituals, in and of themselves, may elicit the undeliberated emotional responses in which a brush with Divinity may be felt and subsequently interpreted. Not to be overlooked is the fact that the way those separate liturgical building blocks are assembled to form the whole worship service is integral to the spiritual experience that will reverberate in one's being after leaving the sanctuary. If you want to maximize the possibility of a heartfelt, meaningful experience, it is important that the progression of liturgical elements is couched in a flow of emotional energy that sustains the intended purpose of each element.

Perhaps you are more familiar with the times when this doesn't happen than how to ensure that it does. Some worshippers will enter into the worship space with something other than giving thanks and praise to God on their minds. Sadly, because nothing that happens in the service is emotionally powerful enough to pull them away from the mundane and toward the divine, they are able to move through the worship experience without ever really shifting their focus away from the distractions they brought with them into the space. The order of worship is so predictable that their hearts, minds, and bodies are never lifted out of the rut of the routine. Whether they are consumed by the argument they had with their adolescent child about coming to church, a problem that awaits them at work the next morning, or a difficult after-church meeting they need to lead, nothing within the worship service breaks the hold these realities have on them. There is no spontaneous emotional experience that might liberate them from the prison of their own thoughts.

Nonetheless, even given the truth that each worshipper carries a different catalog of distractions into the worship experience, the way to seize their attention is not to flood the space with randomly placed stimuli. The way to usher worshippers to the threshold of a God-encounter is to carefully and prayerfully construct pathways that lead them away from distractions and into a communal journey to the altar of Wonder.

Worship planners and leaders who rarely change the order of worship are probably not being attentive to the emotional flow of worship. Just as when you knock on the door of someone who has just landed the job of their dreams versus knocking on the door of a dear friend who suffered the loss of a child, designing a worship experience that invites worshippers into joyful celebration or comfort when coping with tragedy requires a sensitivity to the context of life within and beyond the walls of the sanctuary, remembering that the goal is to create the space for the worshippers to encounter God, flirt with or wallow in thanksgiving and praise, and go forth with hope. Similarly, inviting participation in a worship ritual—whether it is the weekly offering, a foot washing on Maundy Thursday, or an altar call—will be much more encouraging if the emotional energy builds going into that invitation so that the act of engaging in the ritual feels a natural part of the flow of worship.

Especially when I am serving as an interim minister, I often find that I inherit an order of service that does not reflect an attentiveness to worship as an emotional experience. It takes time for me to work with the worship team or the deacons in an effort to adjust the liturgy in a way that may lead the worshippers into a more cohesive, deeper spiritual experience.

In one setting, I inherited the communal expectation that sharing a sign of Christ's peace occurs every week, though often at different points during the worship service. This is the time during the worship service when participants are invited to share a gesture of peaceable, forgiving connection with others in the sanctuary. Those of us who have been a part of this ritual know that it is often much more than that. There is church business being transacted, town gossip being aired, plans being made for later in the day, and medical updates being conveyed. When placed in the middle of the worship service, the intended emotional flow of the worship experience is often disrupted. In an effort to have this burst of communal connection fit better in the whole worship experience, I often (though not always!) place this element toward the beginning of the service. After opening music orients us to the worship experience, the call to worship is spoken or sung and concludes with the invitation to share with one another a sign of Christ's peace. The opportunity to move about and connect with one another, if the Spirit so moves, helps to foster community for that particular worship service. The energy grows and is then harnessed for communal singing as worshippers are asked to join in singing the first hymn.

In another setting, I was told on my very first Sunday as worship leader that I could not make any changes to the order of worship without a vote by the deacons and that I surely would not even approach this subject with them for the first six months. While I accept that there are some who believe that the Christian worship liturgy, just as traditional vocabulary, should never change, I could not abide by this mandate. To do so would show a complete disregard for the truth that encounters with a still-speaking God or living Christ are fluid and organic. They are fleeting manifestations that rise up to meet us in myriad ways, and, gratefully, they are change makers. To keep the worship experience boxed up in a rigid, inflexible liturgy is to deny the Holy Surprise that is born in unexpected places and has the power to transform life.

Jesus taught in boats, on mountaintops, in kitchens, and in the temple courtyard. His tone was sometimes gentle, sometimes bold, sometimes frustrated or invitational, commanding or heartbreaking. He educated, comforted, blessed, directed, promised, and sacrificed. He sought to meet people where they were and take them to a new place of healing, understanding, or hope. He was providing a model for us, and surely we should exercise the same sensitivity to the needs of our "audience" when planning and leading worship.

Liturgical Mapping

As with other exercises throughout this book, liturgical mapping[1] can be done by the pastor alone if she or he is the only planner and leader of worship. However, doing this exercise with a worship team, a board of deacons, or even with an ad hoc group of members who are interested in worship planning may be a way to introduce new ideas and understandings to the congregation as well as reap the creative and spiritual gifts of a variety of members of the worshipping community.

---

1 26 This exercise is based on Thandeka's notion of graphing the emotional arc of worship. Thandeka, "Regulating Internal States."

*Guiding the Worship Planners' Attention
to the Emotional Flow of Worship*

Gather a small group of individuals interested in worship planning. If possible, involve visual people, verbal people, musical people, traditionalists, and innovators. Christian faithfulness, respectfulness of difference, and the desire and ability to play well with others in the sandbox are helpful too.

Distribute copies of a recent Sunday bulletin to each participant. Ask participants to chart the emotional flow of the worship service, according to their personal experience.

> When is the energy high?
> When is it low?
> How can you tell?
> What causes the energy to ebb and flow (consider music, words, objects, movement, ritual, space, and engagement)?

After a brief period of time, invite the participants to share their liturgical maps with each other and reflect upon the following questions.

How do the maps compare with each other? Listen respectfully to each other's explanations regarding where the maps differ, illustrating the differences among worshippers' experiences.

What does the emotional flow say about the core values of your worship service? On what do you place greater attention (emotional energy)? Lesser attention (emotional energy)?

How does the emotional flow correlate with where you, as worship planners, want to direct the worshippers' attention?

In small groups or individually, ask participants to identify one change they might make to the current liturgy that could enhance the emotional engagement of the worshippers, increasing the possibility of a transformative spiritual experience or God-encounter. Ask that they be realistic, but not narrow-minded; courageous, but respectful.

Attending to the Emotional Flow of Worship

Liturgical mapping may reveal that the ritual of the offering, the reading of scripture, the style of the pastoral prayer, or the formatting of the bulletin are low points in the emotional flow of worship. That is to say, they are the moments when people are tempted to check their cell phones for messages or update their to-do lists or flip through the hymnal. Or this exercise may uncover that a brief, traditional moment in the service, which some may take for granted, is one of the most emotionally engaging elements of the worship liturgy for others. The conversation will invite everyone to look at the service in a new way—as an emotional experience, rich with the possibility of spiritual transformation, instead of as a table of contents for an hour of the day. These conversations can be rich and challenging, as they highlight old traditions that may die hard for some members, question practices that you've relied on and thought were tried and true, and even uncover a complete lack of emotional engagement for the entire service. In the end, the exercise of intentional reflection upon the emotional flow and content of worship, in and of itself, may be an emotional and transformative encounter with the Divine.

7

Attending to Virtual Worship

THE YEAR WAS 2020 CE, which many of us know as the Common Era, but, in this instance, might be known as the Computer Era. Six weeks after I entered a new ministry experience, the COVID-19 pandemic washed over the United States and precipitated drastic, but necessary, safety measures, which included the closure of church buildings and governmental limits on the size of in-person gatherings.

Just a few weeks shy of Holy Week and Easter, worship planners worldwide were pressed into creating virtual worship experiences for the highest holy days of the Christian liturgical year. For some of us, the shift was seismic. While some churches were already using technology to enhance and geographically extend the worship experience, many congregations were still struggling to find funds for reliable sound systems in their sanctuaries. Especially for faith communities on a tight budget, whose membership rolls were heavily weighted with those who grew up and worked their professional lives prior to the digital revolution, technological evolution in the shape and practice of ministry did not have a lot of traction. Some churches were still passing around cassettes and DVDs to homebound members, while others were mired in a multiyear discussion about providing the option of electronic giving to their members. In most of the churches I had served, I thought I was doing a great job if I helped move a congregation to recognize the need for instituting technological advances in their ministries and to identify the people and equipment to make that happen. In other words, I was far from being the person who was ready to tackle the practical application of those aspirations, especially under a pandemic time crunch.

Attending to Virtual Worship

Liberation from Fear and Unknowing

However, I knew that if I were going to pastor my congregation through the turbulent, emotional experience of the pandemic, communal worship would have to anchor us in the loving, strengthening presence of God and one another. Having no experience with the computer technology that would best serve my purpose, for the first couple of weeks of our exile from the church sanctuary, I prepared written prayers, prompts, and reflections; interspersed links to music from the Internet; and prayed that the weekly missive would provide some measure of comfort and invitation to the remote worshippers. It was a stopgap strategy at best, while I and others found our compass and navigated our way to a longer-term alternative.

I needed to figure out how to create a virtual sanctuary, first, and then plan and lead worship for a community that was thrust into a vast landscape of fear and unknowns in their daily living. In so doing, I was liberated from my own ignorance and resistance. With gratitude for those colleagues who were experienced, knowledgeable, and willing to share, I wove together webinars, Internet searches, and virtual meetings with peers to create a crash course for myself in offering online worship opportunities. Of course, the options were endless if I wanted to keep on digging. More than once, I had to come up for air from the overwhelming array of choices and the temptation to compare what others were doing to what I and the church I was serving could execute, given all the givens.

My tether through it all was the same commitment that informed my worship planning and leadership prior to our exile—*to create the space for a change of heart, a felt and transformative God-encounter in the experience of worship.* The only thing that was changing—as significant as it was—was the container in which that experience would occur.

Defining the Worship Space

The pandemic hit just as we were approaching Holy Week in 2020, and I was devastated to lose the engaging and contagious aspects of in-person worship. Sharing the same physical space, participating in a shared Lenten ritual in that space, blending voices in song, and participating in the transformation of the three-dimensional space as we journeyed from the upper room to Calvary and on to the empty tomb were unavailable as markers or points of access to me, as worship planner, and to the worshippers, who were desperately reaching for the anchors of a familiar sacred space and liturgy, while being swept up in the tsunami of chaos and separation that came with the pandemic.

Given that the familiarity and personal connection of the in-person communal worship experience were two of the more significant losses of the exodus to a virtual world, it was important for me to create a virtual sanctuary and worship experience that were shaped, in part, by a certain level of familiarity or predictability and the opportunity to connect in community. That is to say, I had no interest in creating a video of myself leading worship in an empty sanctuary, which could be streamed by anyone, anywhere. Especially during this time of isolation, emotional turmoil, and individual trauma, we needed to have the opportunity to gather, hear each other's voices, see each other's faces, and share a common experience, even if our pews were in dining rooms, living rooms, backyards, and bedrooms that were miles apart.

I was introduced to Zoom by way of collegial meetings that were being offered as support to clergy who were leading local churches. It was reasonably accessible, fit in the church budget, and provided a space for worship participants to gather at their usual Sunday morning meeting time, see each other, and speak with each other, all in real time. Zoom Meetings became our virtual sanctuary, and we made every effort to equip the active members and friends of the congregation with the support they needed to participate via computer, laptop, tablet, or phone. There would be some who simply didn't want to "do virtual church," just as there are others who don't want to spend their Sunday morning getting ready and going out to church. Nonetheless, we made consistent efforts to offer simple instructions for clicking or calling in to worship, and some beautiful friendships were formed between tutors and students of all ages.

Our virtual sanctuary was defined in time and space. We would meet via Zoom Meetings at our regular Sunday morning time. In the midst of what seemed like a daily game of fifty-two-card pickup resulting from the pandemic, we were able to maintain the valuable constant of gathering for Sunday morning worship. It was sacramental, a visible sign of God's abiding grace, during our exile from our historic, brick-and-mortar sanctuary.

Attending to the Language of Virtual Worship

Having chosen the container for worship during the pandemic, I made the decision to stick with Zoom Meetings for the duration of our pandemic virtual worship experience. I could not afford the temptation to invest in the exploration and discovery of other options. My pastoral responsibilities increased exponentially during the pandemic, and I didn't want to increase further the already disproportionate amount of time I was giving to technology.

In addition, once worshippers became familiar with Zoom, we could develop some predictable and familiar touchstones for the worship experience. If attendees had been constantly faced with new parameters, bells, and whistles, the navigational requirements would be distracting, and there would be little hope of moving the assembled community to and through a shared worship experience.

With the change of venue from a three-dimensional space to a flat screen, it was important to approach the language of worship from a fresh perspective. While the challenge for many worship planners and leaders in a traditional sanctuary may be how to augment the spoken word with the languages of music, symbols, and rituals to create the space for worshippers to experience a transformative God-encounter, choosing and translating the most appropriate and effective language on the screen requires a different lens of discernment. Some choices will result in the worship experience being too passive. Other choices will lead to overstimulation. Both extremes will lead to distraction, and the communal pilgrimage of prayer and praise will break down.

The first decision I made was to use PowerPoint as the loom that would hold the weaving of the weekly liturgy. Along with the opportunity to see and hear one another via Zoom Meetings, the ability to screen share meant that worship leaders could project the words, prayers, hymns, scripture, and other pieces of the liturgy as needed, decreasing the number of documents or files that needed to be opened and closed during worship. Embedding pictures and music into the PowerPoint meant fewer clicks to distract both the worshipper and worship leader.

The design of the PowerPoint slides is yet another aspect of communicating with the worshipper. The background color of the slide might reflect the color of the liturgical season, replacing the paraments of the traditional sanctuary. The rich green background of ordinary time gives way to a deep purple for Lent. Geometric designs on the slides can be subtle or bold, expressing comfort or proclamation. The graphics may suggest movement or stillness, joy or sorrow, light or darkness. Lively swirls of reds, oranges, and yellows illustrate the fire of Pentecost. Wheat fronds frame the slides on Communion Sunday, and a rainbow border adorns the slides on Pride Sunday. These visuals are a language all their own, and they are a valuable enhancement, but planning and preparing for the virtual worship experience goes beyond choosing the slide format. Indeed, the aesthetics of the traditional, physical sanctuary are a significant facet of the worship experience. As we've explored in previous chapters, worship is a multifaceted experience, even if projected on a digital screen.

There is no foolproof mix of ingredients to guarantee the experience that worship planners may hope for, but there are some things to keep in mind when designing worship for the virtual sanctuary:

- *A written order of worship is helpful.* Given that some attendees will participate via telephone or cell phone, without access to the visuals used in worship, it is useful to provide an order of worship via email so that as many as possible may have access to the words of prayers, hymns, and readings, as well as a roadmap of what to expect in the service. This also helps to fill the desire some members have for the weekly bulletin.

- *Opening space for visiting is valuable.* Allowing room for attendees to arrive early or linger for a few minutes following worship to visit with church friends nurtures a caring community and makes them feel as if they haven't completely lost their coffee hour conversations.

- *Responsive readings are worthwhile.* While most digital meeting applications do not support communal speaking or singing, responsive readings are a valuable piece of the communal liturgy. Speaking prayers aloud is a different experience than simply reading them to yourself. Having a group of people who share one microphone represent the many voices who speak antiphonally with the worship leader creates a call and response so they do not feel as if they are worshipping alone.

- *Music is still the "language of emotion."* Until the digital meeting applications can accommodate live communal singing, the loss of singing together in real time is significant. It is nonetheless important to draw from a variety of sources and styles so that the language of music—the rhythms, mood, quality, and content—support the overall intentions of the worship experience. A recording of their own church choir singing a familiar hymn, an exquisite professional recording of an emotional song, or a single bugle playing taps on Memorial Day can draw one and many into an emotional God-encounter, even in cyberspace.

- *Pictures take us places in our hearts and imaginations.* The virtual sanctuary beckons us to make use of images in worship, which is both gift and temptation. The gift is to share an image that may move us in a profound and unique way. The temptation is to illustrate every prayer, thought, and tune, as if the slideshow were a picture book intended to feed a hungry mind. Even with this expanded bandwidth for presentation, the primary goal is not to entertain, but to lead the worshipper into a particular experience of the Holy. Overstimulation is wasteful, as the brain cannot process two things at once, cognitively or emotionally. Anytime photos or works of art are projected, it's important to allow a moment of quiet for the images to register before speaking or continuing in another way.

- *Rituals require preparation.* While the contagion of sharing rituals in person is significantly compromised in a virtual sanctuary, that is no reason to dispense with all attempts to engage in communal rituals. Inviting worshippers to prepare an altar space wherever they are setting up to attend worship allows them to act in concert with other worshippers, even if separated physically. For example, worshippers preparing their own tables for Communion offers the opportunity to use a cup, plate, and elements that are meaningful for them. Perhaps they will include a candle, a photo, or an icon. If in gallery view during the service of Communion, they will witness and participate in the sacrament as the gathered body of Christ. When inviting worshippers to prepare for a shared ritual, the invitation and guidance should be included in the order of worship that is distributed at least a day before the scheduled worship time.

Ultimately, the design of worship for the virtual space ought to be informed by the same goals of worship in a traditional space. The caution is to avoid overproducing the experience. The joy is to witness how different forms of expression in the virtual sanctuary can lead to profound spiritual experiences, individually and in community.

This Time with Feeling

Creating the Space for Epiphanies in Virtual Worship

With a commitment to the anchors of gathering together, telling stories, and marking time in Christian community, even while exiled from the sacred table and pews that played host to such sharing for generations, there were blessings revealed in this new platform for communal worship.

Show and Tell

Sometimes visual displays can get lost in a large sanctuary, especially if the displays are built to fill the space and be seen from all angles and distances. One of the blessings of a Zoom Meetings worship experience is that pictures of objects and of people can be seen up close and personal on the screen. I saw this as a precious opportunity to invite worshippers to share pictures and stories, offering a reflection of their spiritual journeys. I issued an invitation to church members in advance of planning a particular worship service and asked them to share one or more photos relating to a specific experience or topic: a cherished creche or Advent wreath, a special and memorable meal, or a personally tended garden. In addition, I asked them to write a brief reflection in response to a prompt I gave them. Why is this creche or Advent wreath special to you? How did you see or experience God at the table of a memorable meal? How has your garden testified to resilience and hope? How does it glorify God? I asked if they would be comfortable sharing their pictures and reflections during worship. Most were. Others would ask me to share for them. The pictures and reflections would be carefully placed throughout the worship experience, and I was always amazed at how different offerings seemed to flow into different pieces of the liturgy—a garden reflection of praise created a call to worship, a description of deep fellowship enjoyed around a loaf of homemade bread introduced Communion. The revelations that rose up from the personal sharing were transformative for individuals and the community.

Special Delivery

Not to be defeated in my effort to honor tangible rituals, even in a virtual space, I enlisted a cohort of "delivery angels" who equipped worshippers with objects for upcoming rituals. Palms were delivered for Palm Sunday, with an invitation and prayer for Holy Week. Star ornaments were delivered for Advent, with an invitation to join us for worship, at which time worshippers would be invited to hold a star ornament and pray for a particular person, situation, or community in need of God's outpouring of love. Each week in Advent, worshippers were subsequently encouraged to stop by the church to hang the star on the Advent prayer tree placed there. Those who could not get to the church building were encouraged to hang it in a special place in their homes. While the idea of making deliveries to all the households could seem daunting, the delivery angels and the recipients were equally moved by the gesture and the participation in the ritual.

Windows to the World

While always being cautious about overindulging in the resources at hand when planning a virtual worship experience, there are times when the opportunity to open windows to the world beyond the local church community and experience provides connections and revelations that are transformative. During the pandemic, the community in which I was serving had to cancel their annual in-person Pride gatherings and celebrations. As an Open and Affirming congregation of the United Church of Christ, the congregation usually participated in the parade and festival offerings. When events were cancelled or shifted online, I wanted to be sure our worship experience on Pride weekend was inviting, affirming, and encouraging for present and future partnership with the LGBTQ community. I invited church members to share chapters from their stories of being a member of the LGBTQ community or loving someone who is. I welcomed another church member to share her understanding and passion around the historical context of Pride—its significance in the past and present human experience. Interspersed with those testimonies, we heard the Columbus Gay Men's Chorus sing "We Gotta Pray" by Alicia Keys. We saw the faces and heard the stories of liberating trailblazers for LGBTQ rights, and we put faces to the names of the trans lives lost in 2020. Altogether, the experience was personal and yet so much bigger because the stories of those we knew, who were sitting in our virtual sanctuary, were woven together with the cultural story of which we are all a part.

Illustrated Offerings

Another loss during the extended pandemic season was the ability to make and collect the offering in the traditional way. While some churches may have struggled with the financial ramifications of that omission, I felt it was important to continue the practice of intentional reflection upon our contributions to the gift and responsibility of our covenant with God, one another, and creation. Seizing the moments that might otherwise be used for passing the plate, I would often ask church members to share how they have contributed to human flourishing through their participation in the ministries of the congregation. I would ask them to reflect on what inspired them to participate in this particular ministry of generosity (providing a community meal, being part of drive-by birthday celebrations, making layettes for new mothers in the maternity ward of the local hospitals, assembling bags of essentials for those in need). They would also explain how they had been blessed by their participation. Each week, as a different church member would share their testimony, photos of the activity would be projected on the screen.

As the months passed without the traditional rituals and expressions of faith housed in the historic brick-and-mortar sanctuary and the initial mourning of this lost space ended, it was not unusual to hear members say that they were going to miss worship on the Zoom Meetings platform when the pandemic ended. Even as worshippers were separated by roads and walls, surprisingly, Zoom worship started to feel more intimate than in-person worship in a sanctuary where scores of worshippers were dispersed in a space that held hundreds, and they sat in *their* pews, looking at the backs of the heads of those in front of them. Not only did the personal photos and stories help the worshippers get to know one another and witness the activity of God in their lives, but in gallery view on Zoom they would find themselves sitting beside someone different each week. They could see the faces and expressions of most of those attending. It had the feel of worshipping in a circle, and people grew closer to one another as a result of being thrust into this new way of gathering to worship God.

Looking Forward

More than once, as we endured the exodus experience of the pandemic, venturing into the unknown, but nonetheless hopeful and trusting that we were being led by God, I sought the company and wisdom of another band of faithful that set out on a trek away from their familiar way of life into the horizon of a new way of being—the ancient Israelites. Along the way, these people discovered a nourishing purpose for the quail and manna that were given to them by God as essential sustenance for the journey. I imagine the generation of Hebrews who entered the Sinai desert railed against Moses and God as they choked down the strange, flakey manna again or a random feather with their quail, all the while pining for the days of old: brutal, but familiar and a bit more palatable. The next generation grew up experiencing this foreign meal plan as normal and native. And then the generations that followed praised God for this food because it had sustained their ancestors in a victorious journey to freedom. Forty years in the desert for the Hebrews was not about suspending old ways of being until they could reach safe ground and resume old habits. Forty years in the desert meant that their whole understanding of themselves, what they required, and what was possible would change forever, or at least until the next wilderness sojourn.

Technology is to twenty-first-century churches what manna was to the ancient Israelites. Many churches had resisted embracing, or even imagining, how technology could strengthen their ministries and help them grow into God's dream for the beloved community. Now, as congregations have tasted the possibilities of virtual church, they are ready to make it part of their regular diet. Soon enough, churches that are thriving will be the ones that have adapted not just to using but to relying on the technology that has powered communication and experiences outside the church for decades. For many of us, however, we still must navigate through the wilderness to discover what will work best for our communities of faith.

Our Zoom Meetings worship welcomed people from all around the globe into our virtual sanctuary—long-time members who had retired to another state, family members of church members, church seekers in town or out of town, church members who have health or mobility challenges that keep them at home, and more. This fundamental shift in the way we shape and experience the worshipping community will change church ministry forever. That delights me and concerns me.

I am grateful that we have opened the vault of resources that holds technology and begun to realize how modern modes of communication can exponentially increase our capacity to be church in the world. I can admit that, as much as I choked on the idea of virtual church when it was the only way forward through the pandemic, I have discovered some delectable enhancements to the worship experience, and I love the people I have come to know in cyberspace. But I think the key to moving forward faithfully is to be mindful about how we incorporate technology into the full experience of being church. While church members may be thrilled to throw open the virtual portals and welcome in the world, church pastors may be a bit more cautious. I have only just begun to pray my way into the sea of emerging questions, but they tend to revolve around two fundamental concerns: what the congregation's expectations for the pastor will be, and how we will define our congregations in the future.

How Will Pastoral Roles and Responsibilities Change?

During the pandemic, I sacrificed a lot of time to the technical side of planning and leading virtual worship. Some of that time was my regularly scheduled time off, and some of it was time I would have spent on other important ministries of the church—making pastoral care visits, building partnerships in the community, keeping in touch with the people and pulse in the neighborhood, pouring prayerful and creative energy into discerning how God may be calling us to meet the needs on both sides of the church door. Will churches be willing to swap out the personal interaction and pastoral care they have expected from their ministers in the past for tech prep time in the future?

One way most churches try to support the pastor is by having "technical deacons," members of the church who are comfortable handling the technology needs for worship. However, many churches will struggle to find these human resources within their congregation. And these are likely to be the same churches that aren't prepared or able to spend money for a staff person dedicated to this purpose. Does that mean the pastor will be expected to be the worship IT specialist, as well as worship planner and leader?

How Will Virtual Worship Define the Congregation of the Future?

Sometimes the enthusiasm for developing a virtual worship ministry strikes me as the twenty-first-century version of "We should host a daycare program in our church because it will grow our church membership!" In fact, the numbers have shown repeatedly that housing a daycare program in a church building rarely correlates to an increase in young families joining the church.

On the one hand, I'm all in favor of any welcome that can be extended to folks to experience worship, as the possibility of having a transformative God-encounter is the building block for changing individual and communal lives. On the other hand, I believe worship is an engaged, communal experience that is contagious in person and carries the gift and responsibility for further communal transformation. How does a growing virtual congregation impact the shape and substance of a church whose ministry has evolved to nurture the beloved community and be the hands and feet of Jesus in a particular lot of the vineyard?

How to Begin the Conversation?

While there may be great enthusiasm for carrying forward all the silver linings of the pandemic exile to online worship, the discernment process for establishing an ongoing virtual worship ministry that is sustainable and congregationally owned and understood should not be overlooked. The decision making is not the responsibility of any one group. It would be most effective to have an ad hoc team that includes church members who bring different perspectives and gifts to the table, all of whom are able to engage in respectful, open-minded exploration and conversation: worship planners/leaders, proficient information technologists, property stewards, finance stewards, sanctuary stewards, and individuals who express an interest in developing this ministry, as well as a few skeptics.

Some of the questions this group may need to consider include the following:

- Assuming the congregation wants to return to in-person worship in the sanctuary while also maintaining some form of access for virtual worshippers, what are the goals of holding this hybrid worship experience?

- How do these goals inform the platform and design of the hybrid worship experience?

- How will the shift to hybrid worship impact the pastor's responsibilities for worship preparation and leadership and be balanced against the pastor's other duties?

- What are the copyright issues that need to be considered every week, and who manages these?

- Whose property is the content of the worship service once it has been publicly streamed?
- How will the physical sanctuary need to be added to or remodeled for accommodating hybrid worship needs? What new equipment will need to be purchased, installed, and maintained?
- How does the scope and substance of a church's ministry change when the worshipping community grows in cyberspace beyond those who live locally?
- What does active membership or affiliation in the local church look like, and how does that impact the stewardship of resources?
- Are people who only worship virtually still expected to contribute to sustaining a church building and the ministries that serve the local community?

Having witnessed the daily miracles of people of all ages adapting to virtual sanctuaries, meetings, prayer and book groups, Bible studies, and coffee hours, I am filled with hope for a future in which the blessings of technology are merged with the sacred space of physical sanctuaries and time-honored traditions. I am also fully supportive of nurturing the breadth of God's beloved community as far we can extend it. However, I have also witnessed how difficult conversations can be when the change being discussed is about something as simple as a carpet or cushion color. The profound changes that many churches will experience if the virtual world is invited into a traditional worship setting will very quickly move beyond a joyful celebration of Florida friends being able to worship with their California church community.

I can't help but think that there's a deeper level of discernment that needs to inform decisions about how we utilize this newfound power. I look forward to continuing the conversation with my siblings in faith and with our still-speaking God, Giver of All Good Gifts—manna and technology included!

Benediction

THIS EXPLORATION OF WORSHIP planning and leadership began with the Call to Worship, and so it concludes with the commissioning blessing that is the Benediction. Take yourself to the Mount of Transfiguration. Jesus invites his closest buddies, Peter, James, and John, to take a hike with him. As they sojourn high on a mountain, Peter, James, and John suddenly see Jesus differently, transfigured to look more like an angel and having a conversation with Moses and Elijah. I imagine Jesus then getting peppered with questions as he and his friends walked down the mountain. "What just happened up there?" "How did you do that?" "Was that really Moses and Elijah with you?" "Could everyone see that? Or just us?" "Did you know that was going to happen?" "What does it mean?" Perhaps because he fears they've missed the point, Jesus tells the men not to say a word to anyone about what they saw—at least not for a while.

Peter's immediate response to the vision is priceless. He says to Jesus, "Rabbi, it is good for us to be here; let us make three dwellings, one for you, one for Moses, and one for Elijah" (Mark 9:5). Build dwellings!? For two people who are dead and one he knows isn't going to stay up there? What was he thinking? If we pause to remember what Peter has recently experienced, his response might become clearer.

Just days earlier, Peter dares to call Jesus the Messiah and gets reprimanded for saying so but doesn't get contradicted. Then he hears that this teacher, healer, man of miracles, son of God, is going to be put to death just when things are getting started. And now, on a typical retreat to the mountain, he finds himself in the midst of a communion of saints too great to fathom. And every time he has an aha-moment, Jesus tells him not to talk about it!

There's got to be something that Peter can do to steady this ship, tidy up the confusion, and relieve his distress. "Build dwellings! Yes, we can build dwellings. Keep Jesus safe . . . out of harm's way. The teaching and healing can continue, and the wisdom of the ancient leaders will be honored and available to us 24/7." In the midst of the ambiguity of recent days, Peter was eager to do something, anything, that would help him feel as if the ground beneath his feet would stop shifting. In his desire to bring some order to the chaos and put everything, or everyone, in its place, he reached for the certainty of the familiar, the simple, the concrete.

Faithful members of mainline Protestant churches are feeling very much like Peter these days. The landscape of Christian belief and practice in the United States is changing. The solid ground of Christian worship and community that was the natural gathering place in neighborhoods throughout the middle of the twentieth century has become parched, less fertile for nurturing spiritual life, and is eroding under the constructs that eager believers have built over the centuries, constructs that enshrine particular expressions of faith from a specific time. The language—words, music, symbols, and ritual—of worship has not kept pace with the expressions and experiences of those who might come to know God in a new time and place. As a result, the population inside churches is often a shrinking remnant of the baby boomer generation longing for the good ol' days.

As the number of pledging units and Sunday school enrollees diminishes and budgets are increasingly difficult to balance, that generation of spiritual pilgrims takes a deep dive into survival mode. Some fear the loss of the Christian community that has abided with them from generation to generation and been the center of their communal life. Others are saddened by what they observe as an erosion of faith in God and community, leading to a loss of resiliency that lifts us into hope when we are faced with our greatest challenges. In an effort to shore up their ranks, solidify their place in the culture, and securely anchor themselves in a rapidly changing world, they're attention shifts to building dwellings that capture and preserve a bygone era, sheltering them against the winds of change. The buildings, the pews, the words, the liturgy, the rituals, the organizational structure, and sometimes even the strawberry suppers and Christmas fairs are among the givens and, as one generation after another institutionalizes its belief and practice, there is less space for the living to dance with the Spirit. Alas, petrification that is fear begets the petrification that is the loss of life. An exciting movement fueled by encounters with the living Christ atrophies into a museum, albeit with loving and well-meaning docents.

Benediction

But what happens when we prayerfully and attentively seek to create an *experience* of worship rather than simply a *service* of worship? What happens when we dare to dismantle some of our human constructs rather than reflexively reinforce them without careful consideration of the ways they welcome or exclude seekers and believers in the twenty-first century? What happens when we *feel* our way into God-encounters that have the power to transform us, as individuals and as communities?

Creating the space in worship for a felt experience of God changes the way worshippers anticipate worship, it changes the way they experience worship, and it changes what they take away from worship. Instead of knowing exactly what's going to happen, they come with heightened expectations of the unexpected. Not unlike being attentive to God-sightings in the balance of their lives, they attend worship believing that they may be surprised by the Holy and they assume a posture of active waiting. Something exciting, powerful, or new and relevant may unfold in the sacred space of a sanctuary and sixty minutes. An engaging experience awaits them, which requires them to be more than passive observers. They will be called upon to be co-creators of this worship experience—participating in a ritual, engaging in a communal conversation, exercising their imagination, prayerfully sharing their cares and joys with the community, and experiencing the Jesus story in a moving way. On a blessed day, they leave the sanctuary having experienced a change of heart, an aha-moment, or a transformative communion with Hope, Peace, Beauty, or God. And, if so inspired and encouraged, they talk about it. They tell their own story of God's activity in their lives, and it changes the way they act and interact in the world.

The encounter with Jesus, glorified, and Moses and Elijah, wasn't about the three pillars of the faith shown in a new light. It was about the three disciples and how their perception and belief would be forever altered by that encounter. Climb the mountain—or at least take the first step. Pay attention and see the possibilities for creating the worship *experience* in a new light—this time with feeling!

Appendix 1

Reimagining Psalm 23 in the Context of an Infant's Baptism

GOD IS LIKE YOUR favorite blanket. Always wrapped around you, God will answer to the name you call. God will pacify you. God will warm you. God might even trip you up when you take your first steps, but only for the good. God's strong finger is always held out for you to hold on to.

God takes you to your favorite napping places and gives you creative solitude in the sandbox. God heals booboos and makes everything better, all in due time. In baptism, we celebrate that God has given you a heart that has the capacity to learn right from wrong and what is holy.

Hunger and thirst, teething, and boogie monsters have nothing on God. God gives you baby biscuits and mother's milk, rocking chairs, and musical mobiles to calm you.

Even when you feel like you're all alone and you wonder why no one seems to understand your desperate pleas over the airwaves of a monitor, you will be surprised by the distraction of a daydream or the friendship of a sock monkey.

Spontaneous smiles and uncontrollable giggles will be sprinkled upon your days and, at the very least, when you are among this church family, we hope you will know Love.

Appendix 2

Centering Ourselves in the Generosity and Forgiveness of God

The Week after Easter

EASTER DINNERS, EASTER BASKETS, Easter egg hunts, and Easter blessings; sugaring, raking, planting starters for the vegetable and flower gardens, laying mulch, and sweeping sand; feeling the weariness and the pressure of a school year two thirds gone, anticipating April vacation, sensing spring fever beginning to percolate in the office, and staring down the due dates for taxes. In the midst of it all, birdsong grows louder, stale air makes way for fresh air, and longer and sunnier days put a spring in our steps. Seize this moment to pause. Take a deep, slow, cleansing breath, and turn your attention toward the good things, good places, and good people in your life. Replace the hurriedness with thankfulness. Replace the pressure with gratitude. Replace your thoughts about what's missing with thoughts about the Good that is there.

(Pause for silent reflection.)

It is easy to forget to name and give thanks for our blessings in the fullness of our daily lives. So too, it is easy to dismiss those situations that beg us to try again after failing, say I'm sorry after offending, forgive after being hurt. Pause in this moment to plant your own starters, seed your own new life in spring, that you may right your relationships with God, with parents, siblings, friends, coworkers, strangers, and with the land and waters, flora and fauna of creation.

(Pause for silent reflection.)

Centering Ourselves in the Generosity and Forgiveness of God

As we come to the table of Generosity and Forgiveness, invited to fill our own chalices so that we might then pour them out for others, we echo the prayer that Jesus taught us, using our own words. (The Lord's Prayer)

For Use in an Intergenerational Context

I invite you to sit quietly, close your eyes if that's comfortable for you, and follow my lead as we center ourselves in the generosity and forgiveness of God.

What have you experienced this week that makes you want to say "thank you"? What were you doing? Who were you with? How did you feel?

(Pause for silent reflection.)

What have you done or said this week that makes you want to say "I'm sorry"? What were you doing? Who were you with? How did you feel?

(Pause for silent reflection.)

When we say "thank you," when we apologize, and when we accept someone else's apology, God blesses us. Whether we feel thankful and happy or we feel sad, lonely, or angry, we can come together and find just the right words as we pray the prayer that Jesus taught us. (The Lord's Prayer)

Appendix 3

Prayers for End-of-Life Services

Opening Words at a Funeral

READING: PSALM 100

If you have ever been greeted by "Connie," you know the joy and gladness of which the psalmist speaks. Put another way, the psalmist says, "Give it up for God. You are blessed. You have the divine breath of life in you. The carpet of God's creation has been rolled out for you and you will always and forever stand in God's love, surprised by it in both understated and lavish ways." As I said, if you have ever been greeted by "Connie," you know the joy and gladness of which the psalmist speaks. With every encounter, there was always a bright glimmer of recognition, accompanied by a sincere and focused connection that conveyed how pleased she was to see you and how concerned she was about your whereabouts and your happiness. Somehow, she made you feel special and even helped you realize how blessed you are.

It is true that we gather today to experience the grace of community during a time of loss. It is true that the void left on this earth by "Connie's" leave-taking; the concern for her husband, John; and the meanderings of our hearts and minds to other losses, past or present, can leave us with a very somber spirit. But, if we pause to imagine "Connie" approaching any one of us even now, in this moment, smiles would ripple through this place we call sanctuary and the spirit would not be a somber one.

I invite you to take a moment now to greet one another with the generosity of spirit that was "Connie's."

Prayers for End-of-Life Services

A Prayer Written for a Family Gathered at the Bedside of a Dying Wife and Mother

The family members were of different Christian faith denominations. The husband/father was a retired UCC clergyman who described himself and his wife as "post-theists."

Dwelling in the Holy

Hymn: "Spirit of the Living God"

Jesus said, "For where two or three are gathered in my name, I am there among them."

Unison Response: Love, Peace, Comfort, come.

This is a culminating moment in a sacred journey. It is a unique communion of hearts and souls gathered here, in person and in Spirit, drawn together by the life and love of a woman we have known as wife and mother, friend, and teacher. However, as we call out to the Embrace of the Universe, we can know that this journey into death and new life is one that's been traveled by One and many. The Grace that allows us to be one with another, even now, is here, and we are grateful.

Unison Response: Calm, Trust, Strength, come.

Thoughts spoken and unspoken, gestures extended and imagined, feelings named and unnamed; the altar in this moment is where we stand, sit, and lie. It is where blessings have been offered and received. Here we have pondered, prayed, and given thanks. We have remembered, planned, and loved. We have laughed, cried, and held caring, silent vigil. It has been our nourishment, our sanctuary, our worship.

Unison Response: Beauty, Solace, Understanding, come.

Thanksgiving

For the chalice of life that has held "Anne," we are eternally grateful. It is a body that has been a vessel of Strength, Grace, Wisdom, Love, Life, Creativity, Compassion, and Honesty. Through the Generous Miracle that is life incarnate, we are grateful for the enduring imprints she has left on our lives and the lives of family, friends, students, and strangers.

(As the Spirit moves, those gathered might share in words or phrases the imprints "Anne" has left on them.)

Appendix 3

Now, while her spirit flies free, we appreciate that her body will continue to teach. Opportunities for life and learning still flow from this chalice, even now. For "Anne's" ongoing contributions to this earthly life and for those who know how to reap the knowledge from her gift that can change and mend lives, we give thanks.

Abiding Grace

As we part, we pray.
Shadow us, Grace, in our uncertainty.
Accompany us, Love, in our loneliness.
Flow through us, Forgiveness, in the painful places of loss.
Surprise us, Laughter, in our storytelling.
Cradle us, Peace, in our sleepless nights.
Lead us, Gratitude, in our looking back and our looking ahead.
Meet us, Patience, in our slowness to heal.

And, when words don't come easily, yet our pleas beg to be voiced, allow us to rely on the prayer of our tradition, using our own words. (The Lord's Prayer)

Commendation

Life dispensed and disbursed
In one form, finite; in many ways, eternal
Blessed and Blessing
Holy and Human
Created and Creating
The journey into the Mystery continues.
Unison Response:
Love, Peace, Comfort, come.
Calm, Trust, Strength, come.
Beauty, Solace, Understanding, come.
Carry her with Gentleness and Reverence.

Continue to pour her life from this chalice, gilding the living with her grace.

Entrusted to all that is Holy, may she be welcomed into the fullness of the Universe, in Peace.

Hymn: "Spirit of the Living God"

Appendix 4

Advent Candle-Lighting Liturgy

Call to Worship and Lighting of the Advent Candle (Week 1)

Leader:
Hope is . . .
a popcorn kernel in a hot pan
a newly planted garden
the first page of a book you want to read
waking up to a foot of snow on a school day
remission
Unison Response:
Hope is . . .
the writer's blank page
a tug on the end of the fishing line
the smell of chocolate chip cookies in the oven
an acorn
Leader:
Hope is . . .
a second chance
opening a new box of crayons
the look in a puppy's eye when you are holding a tennis ball
"I'm sorry"
"I forgive you"

Appendix 4

Unison Response:
Hope is . . .
the angel Gabriel
a courageous woman
Light in the darkness
a baby in the manger
Leader:
Hope is.
And so, we gather for worship. Let us sing.

Call to Worship and Lighting of the Advent Candle (Week 2)

Leader:
Peace is . . .
reconciliation
an autumn afternoon in the hammock
the morning after a ticker tape parade
sometimes a journey through quiet, sometimes not
Unison Response:
Peace is . . .
the moment the baby finally falls asleep
just you, a kayak, and a lazy river
finding unity in diversity
sometimes a rewarding comfort, sometimes not
Leader:
Peace is . . .
a healthy body
a steady heartbeat
a stable mind
consensus
a deep cleansing breath, with a long slow exhale
sometimes easy to find, sometimes not
Unison Response:
Peace is . . .
more than the absence of violence
more than avoiding someone with whom we disagree
more than bringing order to the chaos

Advent Candle-Lighting Liturgy

Leader:
Peace is . . .
couched in the wisdom of the prophets
a lion and a lamb
a baby who grew up a rebel
a Holy and Human work in progress
Unison Response:
Peace is possible.
And so, we gather for worship. Let us sing.

Call to Worship and Lighting of the Advent Candle (Week 3)

Leader:
Joy looks like . . .
a dog's wagging tail
leaping dolphins
the embraces and faces of a longed-for reunion
a successful exchange of milk and cookies on Christmas Eve for presents on Christmas morn
Unison Response:
Joy smells like . . .
bacon sizzling in the pan
the freshness in the air following a spring rain
sun-drenched cotton sheets
the top of a baby's head
Leader:
Joy sounds like . . .
the Hallelujah Chorus
the purr of a cat
uncontrollable laughter
quiet weeping with amazement
Unison Response:
Joy tastes like . . .
a first kiss
a morning cup of coffee
a snowflake as it melts on your tongue
a cool glass of water on a hot summer day

Appendix 4

Leader:
Joy feels like . . .
exhilaration!
connection!
affirmation!
awe!
Unison Response:
But Joy is . . .
deeper than happiness
more profound than satisfaction
a note that reverberates through your whole being
Leader:
Joy is . . .
manna from heaven
the gift of sight to a blind man
mourning turned into dancing
Unison Response:
Emmanuel, God with us
Joy rekindles Hope for Peace.
And so, we gather for worship. Let us sing.

Call to Worship and Lighting of the Advent Candle (Week 4)

Leader:
If you have . . .
sat through a game even though you don't like sports
made a gift with popsicle sticks and dry elbow macaroni
prepared a meal even though cooking is not your strong suit
or risked failure to grow with another
you have known what Love is.
Unison Response:
If you have . . .
been grateful to call someone "family," by birth or by choice
intervened, with Courage and Grace, in someone's addiction
swung the hammer for Habitat
shed tears for the hurts of another
or experienced forgiveness

Advent Candle-Lighting Liturgy

you have known what Love is.
Leader:
If you have . . .
sacrificed the last bite of your meal to your partner or pet
accompanied someone taking a last breath
found your way back after being miles apart
or allowed romance to trump all else
you have known what Love is.
Unison Response:
Love Is . . .
God poured out
in Jesus
in you
and in me.
Leader:
Love is at hand.
And so, we gather for worship. Let us sing.

Appendix 5

Worshippers Participating in the Drama of Jesus' Last Days

Standing at the Edge of the Procession

I ASKED PEOPLE, INCLUDING children, to imagine themselves at the edge of Jesus' procession into Jerusalem. What would they say? How would they feel? Here are some of their responses, which were part of an unfolding drama in the Palm/Passion Sunday worship service.

Response #1

From the children (edited from a conversation in church school):

The other day we were talking with some of our friends and some of our parents were around. Somebody asked us, "If you were to meet Jesus today, if he were right in front of you, and you could say anything or ask anything, what would you say to Jesus?"

Many of the younger kids said that they'd "be scared and run home" if they encountered Jesus. One of them said, "I'd faint."

The oldest kids didn't even want to believe it. At first, they just said that it wouldn't or couldn't be Jesus. They wanted to know for sure. They wanted proof. One of my friends said, "How would we know it was really him? He'd have to prove it." Another one just thought it would be weird.

But some of us did have questions or thoughts that we would share with Jesus. This is what some of them were.

"Thank you for all you've done for us."

"What am I going to get for my birthday?"
"I don't think he'd speak English, do you?"
"Do dogs go to Heaven too?"
"Will animals ever be able to speak?"
"What is my dog thinking?"
"Will we eventually reach world peace?"
"I know I can't change anything about the world; I guess it just has to come out how it does."
"Where will my life take me? How will it be different from now?"
"Will I see you again?"
"Can I talk to you again?"
"I would immediately think I must have done something very very bad for Jesus to show up."
"What's my future?"
"Why is the world like this?"
"Why do you have time to talk to me?"
And then even the grown-ups had some questions that they would ask.
"Why do some people have lots of food and others have none?"
"Why do you still love us even though sometimes—lots of times—we're not very good?"
"Why do some people suffer and others don't?"
"Do dogs have souls?"
And when one of my friends said she wouldn't have anything to say, her mother said, "What? It's Jesus. I'll prod you to say something, anything." Eventually, my friend said, "Okay. I would say, 'Jesus, can you please come to my house? I don't have anything to say to you, but my mom has *a lot* to talk to you about.'"

Response #2

From an older woman, once a Quaker, now an active member of this UCC church:

Who is this? Why are people greeting this simple-looking man as though he were a king? Oh, there he is. Wow. Look at his face. You can see his humility. He's looking at us with this peaceful knowingness and in such a loving way. I can really sense his strength and goodness. Who is this?

Appendix 5

Response #3

From young parents, whose faith expression didn't always fit within the frame of tradition, but who wanted to teach their children about Jesus:

Parent 1: Come on, everyone! Have you heard? Jesus is coming! To our town! We might actually get a chance to see him.

Child 1: Who?

Parent 2: Jesus of Nazareth. It would be great if we could see through this crowd. I've heard so much about him. I never thought I'd get to see him in person.

Kid 1: Where's the parade? Will he be riding in a fancy chariot? I bet all the really cool people will be with him.

Parent 1: Not Jesus. That isn't really his style. He spends his time with a lot of people who would surprise you—children, tax collectors, lepers, poor people, sinners. He even eats meals with them and spends time in their homes. He keeps saying that we are all children of God—that we're all important and deserve to be cared for.

Kid 1: Oh, I know who you mean! He's that guy who did all the miracles!

Parent 2: That's the one. He helped the paralyzed man to walk, made a blind man see, and even brought one of his friends back from the dead. He fed a huge crowd with just a few loaves and fishes.

Kid 2: I heard he can walk on water!

Parent 1: All those things are incredible, but it's what he's teaching that makes me want to see him. His message is what is really important.

Parent 2: He teaches that we should love each other—not just those who love us, but everyone. He says that we should take care of each other—especially the poor. He wants us all to be peacemakers. He says we should speak the truth and that we should believe in him, even if others hold that against us.

Kid 1: Why would anyone hold that against us?

Parent 1: It's not an easy lesson for some people. Jesus speaks about the kingdom of God, and I want to be a part of that.

Kid 1: I don't think I understand all of that.

Parent 1: Neither do I, but I think we should keep trying. Let's try to get closer and hear what he has to say.

Worshippers Participating in the Drama of Jesus' Last Days

Response #4

From a lifelong believing and thoughtful Christian man:

Some of my friends said we should go to see this person whom some call the Messiah, or maybe he is Elijah. I don't know. He seems to be a modest person. Like me, on a donkey, not very grand. I'm not very grand myself. I think if I stand at the edge of this crowd, the kind of crowd that looks at the Romans march past, nobody will notice me. Safer to be at the back than at the front. All of a sudden everybody is getting excited. They're shouting at him to save us. "Hosanna!" What's that all about? I don't know, but I might as well join in. Don't want to be too different, just left alone, here on the edge.

Response #5

From a young woman discovering her faith:

Dear God,

Thank you for the hosannas and the praise.

Thank you for pulling me from my thoughts into the present moment, a present moment that consists of celebration and happiness.

Help me to recognize the significance of each moment. This moment when we remember Jesus' entry into Jerusalem amidst cheers and fanfares is so obvious and clear. But bring me back to the moment even when it is subtler and its transforming power could easily be overlooked, crowded out by thoughts and concerns of future tasks and worries.

Help me to share this moment with others: with my family, friends and public. Help me find a way to express the joy that comes from learning from Jesus, learning the value of his teachings, stories, and love.

So, thank you for this initial celebration. Let it not be overshadowed by the serious events of the week to come right now. Let the joy and praise sink into me. Praise and amen.

Response #6

Two different perspectives from women on the Board of Deacons:

Woman 1: Why is he getting so much attention. Who is he? Isn't he just that guy that we've known since he was a kid?

Appendix 5

Woman 2: This man is very special—full of God's spirit, and who shares that spirit with all. Some even say he is God's son.

Response #7

From a courageous, poetic academic who grew up in the Roman Catholic tradition:

He thrust a palm branch in my hand,
His eyes dancing,
His face contorted in a hope-filled grin.
Fool.
To think this parading peasant could conquer the Empire.
The prophecy is wrong.
they will strike his head,
And with the heel of their boots they will grind you all
to dust.

Response #8

An ordained UCC clergyman, retired from parish ministry, who considers himself a "post-theist," selected an excerpt from the Gospel of Andrew, with some adaptation:

Hello. I am Andrew of Bethsaida.

Of all of the twelve disciples closest to Jesus, Philip and I were most influenced by Greek culture and philosophy. There was a very strong Greek influence in the town of Bethsaida where we grew up and worked before joining up with Jesus. So, my experience and understanding of Jesus came through the influence of that Greek culture almost more than from Hebrew ways of religion. Actually, the three Greek men who were there in Bethany, as mentioned in John's Gospel, were friends of mine from Bethsaida. They realized that events were approaching a crisis as Jesus prepared to enter Jerusalem in that week before Passover. They knew that they might not have another chance to speak to Jesus directly, and they had one particular question to ask him. They thought that Jesus might be able to bridge the fundamental divide between religion and philosophy. So, when I took my Greek friends over to where Jesus was, I knew what they wanted to ask Jesus because we had talked about it many times in Bethsaida. The question was this: is the spiritual experience of God and the experience of love totally equivalent so that to say God and Love has identical meaning? In other words, for you, Jesus, is the experience of God and the experience of Love essentially the same, and the way to abundant life and fulfillment for all?

So how did Jesus answer those Greeks? He said, "You got it, man!!! That's it! Now, as Greeks, don't just think about *Love* or just write philosophy about *Love*, but go out and *Do It*."

At the Edge of the Last Supper

"Last Lunch," by a Young Woman Who Loves Jesus

I can't envision being at the last supper, but I can envision a last lunch—where Jesus stops by for some soup with me and some women friends. I offer him a spoonful of my chicken noodle soup with chanterelle mushrooms and arugula—with a savory broth I let simmer for two full days. He closes his eyes and says, "This is good," and in his voice, just for a moment, it's as if I hear Creator God moving over the waters on the brink of dazzling invention. I hear . . . let there be light! Then in Spanish, then in French, then in Aramaic, Arabic, and Swahili, then in languages I can't even name—let there be cooking and laughing and gardening and skiing. Let there be stories and salamanders and snow and whole worlds of glow-in-the-dark creatures in the deep sea.

I see an image of clay people from an Aztec creation story—clay people who stir and open their eyes when the Spirit of God breathes life into their clumsy forms. I look down at my hands for a moment. Heavy they seem today, as I stand near Jesus. He's leaning against the cabinet tasting my soup, and I have a terrible feeling of dread, as if this will be the last time I have conversation with him like this, in my kitchen.

I offer him some bread for the soup. And turn to cut off some pieces of cheese.

He breaks the bread, hands me half of it, and says something cryptic about this is my body broken for you. There's a solemnity in his voice, but also something else, something I can't name and a kind of light in his eyes, as if he knows some wonderful secret better than any I've ever known.

I'd have to not know it was the last time he'd be in my kitchen; otherwise, I'd have the inclination to hide him, to not let him make his way to the cross, to not let him leave us. "Stay and play cards!" I might say, or "Let's read some poetry—you are always telling me to sit still, to slow down, that I busy myself too much."

Don't go.

I might act rashly, suspecting that he was in danger. Rome was unhappy by all this trouble, all the prophecies and these miraculous stories. Perhaps he should have hidden his powers. He should not have touched the blind man, the leper, or that dead girl and Lazarus. It was too much. He should not be telling stories about the kingdom of God as if he had authority to do so and knowledge of such a kingdom. He upset the powers that be. He should have kept a lower profile. Maybe I could hide him here in the extra bedroom. As much as I like to think I'd be considering the bigger picture, I'd likely be focused on the now and living mostly blind in the smaller story, unable to envision the larger story that Christ would open up by dying on the cross.

At the Edge of the Crowd Witnessing the Crucifixion

From a Young Father and Entrepreneur

Holding a grudge is like letting someone live rent free in your head. Instead of doing so, we must join his group of followers. Jesus was crucified for being at the edge, where all ideas and movements by definition begin. But the first follower moved him from isolation, and each additional follower adds to his credibility and slowly but surely will push his message from the edge to the center.

Bibliography

Armstrong, Karen. *A History of God: The 4,000-Year Quest of Judaism, Christianity and Islam.* New York: Ballantine, 1993.
Brown, Raymond E. *Christ in the Gospels of the Liturgical Year.* Collegeville, MN: Liturgical, 2008.
Chittister, Joan. *Listen with the Heart.* Lanham, MD: Rowman & Littlefield, 2003.
———. *The Liturgical Year: The Spiraling Adventure of the Spiritual Life.* Nashville: Thomas Nelson, 2009.
Connell, Martin J. "The Origins and Evolution of Advent in the West." In *Between Memory and Hope: Readings on the Liturgical Year,* edited by Maxwell E. Johnson, 349–71. Collegeville, MN: Liturgical, 2000.
Eklund, Andy. "How to Use Metaphors to Inspire Creative Thinking." AndyEklund.com. October 14, 2014. http://www.andyeklund.com/metaphors-and-creative-thinking.
Gardner, Howard. *Frames of Mind: The Theory of Multiple Intelligences.* New York: Basic Books, 1983.
Goleman, Daniel. *Focus: The Hidden Driver of Excellence.* New York: HarperCollins, 2013.
Grant, C. David. *Thinking Through Our Faith: Theology for Twenty-First-Century Christians.* Nashville: Abingdon, 1998.
Grotowski, Jerzy. *Towards a Poor Theatre.* New York: Routledge, 2002.
Hanson, Bradley C. *Introduction to Christian Theology.* Minneapolis: Fortress, 1997.
Hickman, Hoyt L., Don E. Saliers, Laurence Hull Stookey, and James F. White. *The New Handbook of the Christian Year.* Nashville: Abingdon, 1992.
Horowitz, Alexandra. *On Looking: A Walker's Guide to the Art of Observation.* New York: Scribner, 2014.
Kaufman, Gordon. *In Face of Mystery: A Constructive Theology.* Cambridge, MA: Harvard University Press, 1995.
———. *In The Beginning . . . Creativity.* Minneapolis: Augsburg Fortress, 2004.
Kavanagh, Aidan. *Elements of Rite: A Handbook of Liturgical Style.* Collegeville, MN: Liturgical, 1990.
———. *On Liturgical Theology.* Collegeville, MN: Liturgical, 1992.
Levine, Peter, with Ann Frederick. *Waking the Tiger: Healing Trauma.* Berkeley, CA: North Atlantic, 1997.
McFague, Sallie. *Metaphorical Theology: Models of God in Religious Language.* Minneapolis: Fortress, 1982.
———. *Models of God: Theology for an Ecological, Nuclear Age.* Minneapolis: Fortress, 1987.

Bibliography

Mendelsohn, Daniel. Lost: *A Search for Six of Six Million*. New York: Harper Perennial, 2013.
Merton, Thomas, and William H. Shannon. *The Inner Experience: Notes on Contemplation*. New York: HarperOne, 2003.
Morley, Janet. *Bread of Tomorrow*. London: SPCK/Christian Aid, 1992.
Panksepp, Jaak, and Lucy Biven. *The Archaeology of Mind: Neuroevolutionary Origins of Human Emotions*. New York: Norton, 2012.
———. "The Emotional Antecedents to the Evolution of Music and Language." *Musicae Scientiae* 13/2 (September 2009) 229–59.
———. "A Synopsis of Affective Neuroscience—Naturalizing the Mammalian Mind." Introduction and discussion in the "The Philosophical Implications of Affective Neuroscience." *Journal of Consciousness Studies* 19/3–4 (2012) 6–18.
Peluso-Verdend, Gary. *Paying Attention: Focusing Your Congregation on What Matters*. Herndon, VA: Alban Institute, 2005.
Schleiermacher, Friedrich. *The Christian Faith*. Berkeley, CA: Apocryphile, 2011.
Schram, Ruth Elaine. *If I Had Been*. Miami: CCP Belwin Mills, 1992.
Stanfield, Burns. "Introduction to the Liturgical Calendar." Lecture delivered in the course "Christianity as a Way of Life: The Liturgical Year" by Andover Newton. Theological School, Newton Centre, MA, February 12, 2014.
Steinbeck, John. *The Grapes of Wrath*. New York: Viking, 1939.
Stone, Howard W., and James O. Duke. *How to Think Theologically*. Minneapolis: Augsburg Fortress, 2013.
Thandeka. "Future Designs for American Liberal Theology." *American Journal of Theology and Philosophy* 30/1 (January 2009) 72–100.
———. "Regulating Internal States." Lecture delivered in the course "Inspiring Worship." Andover Newton Theological School, Newton Centre, MA, October 22, 2015.
———. "Schleiermacher's Affekt Theology." *International Journal of Practical Theology* 9/2 (December 2005) 197–216.
Tillich, Paul. *Dynamics of Faith*. New York: HarperCollins, 2001.
Turner, Edith, with William Blodgett, Singleton Kahona, and Fideli Benwa. *Experiencing Ritual: A New Interpretation of African Healing*. Philadelphia: University of Pennsylvania Press, 1992.
United Church of Christ. "Preamble to the Constitution of the United Church of Christ." http://www.ucc.org/beliefs_preamble-to-the-constitution.
Wilson, Ralph F. "The Day Peter Ran." Joyful Heart Renewal Ministries. http://www.joyfulheart.com/easter/peter-ran.htm.

Index

Abiding Grace prayer, 120
Advent rituals, 81–85, 81n1, 121–25
age-old refrains, 22–24
ancient Israelites, 107
anxiety, 48
Armstrong, Karen, 21n1
artwork of belief, 56, 61–62, 64–67
attendance, 1–2
attentiveness, 8, 13–14, 78

baptism, 115
Benediction, 111–13
biblical images, 25–29
biblical story, 78–79, 85–87
black Americans, 67–68
borrowed words, 34–40

call and response, 36–37, 102
call to worship, 121–25
candle-lighting liturgies, 82–83, 121–25
Centering Ourselves in the Generosity and Forgiveness of God liturgy, 35–36, 116–17
children's message, 4–5, 7, 12, 49
Chittister, Joan, 54, 87
Christ-centered community, 3
Christian belief and practice, 3–4, 18, 28, 69–70, 112
Christian communities, 2–4
The Christian Faith (Schleiermacher), 19
Christian traditions, 20, 34–36, 40–41, 77–81, 83, 87–90
Commendation prayer, 120
Common Era (CE), 3, 77, 90

communal life
  communal prayer, 22–23
  conversation, 113
  emotional flow of worship, 94–95
  Jesus story, 2–3
  virtual worship, 98–110
communication, 21, 45
connection, 1–2, 7. *See also* participation
Connell, Martin J., 81n1
Constantine, 3
contemplation, 47n2
conversations, 5, 69, 102, 109–10, 113
COVID-19 pandemic, 98–110

"The Day Peter Ran" (Wilson), 15–16
delivery angels, 104–5
denominational resources, 38
denominations, 3–4
distractions, 10–11, 93–94
divine awareness, 19
Doing the Best We Can with What We've Got, 43, 51
Dwelling in the Holy prayer, 119
Dynamics of Faith (Tillich), 26n4

Elijah, 111–13
embedded theology, 25–26, 33–34
emotional flow of worship
  liturgical mapping, 95–97
  multiple intelligences, 56
  music, 45–47, 53
  rhythms, 91–92
  still life tableaus, 69–70
  worship experience, 9–10, 14–18, 46–47, 69–70, 92–97

Index

end-of-life services, 38–39, 118–20
Enlightenment, 4
essential gospel, 40–41, 80–81
experience of God, 2, 6–7, 27, 46, 55–56, 113, 130–31. *See also* God-encounters
experience of worship. *See* worship experience

faith experiences, 45–50, 89–90. *See also* worship experience
Fish (Still Life) (Manet), 63
Focus (Goleman), 13
Frames of Mind (Gardner), 56n1
funerals, 38–39, 118

Gardner, Howard, 56n1
gathering together, 76–79, 90. *See also* worship experience
generosity, ministry of, 106
God-encounters
  biblical images, 25–29
  communal prayer, 23
  distractions, 94
  divine awareness, 19
  emotion, 70, 96
  intellect, 11
  language of worship, 23, 41, 85
  liturgical year, 90
  music, 43, 47, 51, 103
  primary theology, 18–19
  spiritual experiences, 9–10
  still life tableaus, 74–75
  symbols, 64
  virtual worship, 99, 101, 103, 109
  worship experience, 56, 93, 95, 99, 103, 109, 113
  worship planning and leadership, 13, 78–79, 99, 101
God is Good . . . All the Time: An Illustration, 36–37
Goleman, Daniel, 13
Grant, C. David, 26n3
The Grapes of Wrath (Steinbeck), 61–62
Great Performances, 42–43, 51

History of God (Armstrong), 21n1

Holy Week, 87–90
Homecoming Sunday, 14
human experience, 6
hybrid worship, 109–10

"If I Had Been" (Schram), 16
illustrated offerings, 106
images of God, 25–29
imagination, 113
individualism, 4
inherited worship traditions, 20
The Inner Experience (Merton), 47n2
intellect, 11, 46, 69
intergenerational conversations, 5
Invaluable Orchestration Partners, 43–44, 47–49

Jesus movement, 3
Jesus story
  Benediction, 111–13
  biblical images, 26
  communal connection, 2–3
  God-consciousness, 19
  liturgical calendar, 77–79, 87–88
  transformative worship, 6
  worshippers participating in drama of last days, 126–32

Kavanagh, Aidan, 18

language of emotions, 45
language of worship, 21–41. *See also* music
  age-old refrains, 22–24
  biblical images, 25–29
  borrowed words, 34–40
  essential gospel, 40–41
  theological terms, 29–34
  worship experience, 85–88
learning styles, 56n1
LGBTQ community, 105
lighting of the Advent candle, 82–83, 121–25
liturgical calendar
  Christian traditions, 77–81
  Holy Week, 87–90
  Jesus story, 77–79, 87–88

Index

language of worship, 85–87
music, 46–47
ritual, 79–81
sensory experience, 89–90
testimonies, 88–89
liturgical mapping, 95–97
Lord's Prayer, 22, 24, 117, 120
Lost: A Search for Six of Six Million (Mendelsohn), 40

mainline Protestant churches, 1–2, 13, 18, 55, 112
Manet, Édouard, 63
marking time, 76–79, 90. *See also* liturgical calendar
Mendelsohn, Daniel, 40
Merton, Thomas, 47n2
metaphors, 27, 28–31
monotheism, 22, 22n2
Moses, 111–13
multiple intelligences, 56
music, 42–54, 84–85, 94–95, 102–3
myths, 26n4

occasional services, 38, 39
offering collection, 106
order of worship, 94–95, 102
"The Origins and Evolution of Advent in the West" (Connell), 81n1

Panksepp, Jaak, 45
participation, 1–2, 23, 60–61, 68–70, 83, 103, 104–6, 112–13, 126–32. *See also* worship experience
pastoral ministry, 19, 108
Peter, 15–16, 111–12
piety, 19
post-resurrection discipleship, 3
post-worship comments, 20
PowerPoint, 101–2
prayers, 22–24, 118–20
"Preamble to the Constitution of the United Church of Christ," 4
Pride weekend, 105
primary theology, 18–20
Protestant Reformation, 11, 55

Protestants. *See* mainline Protestant churches
Psalm 23, 38–39, 115
Psalm 30, 67–68
Psalm 139, 14

rationalism, 4, 69
Reformed worship service, 11
religious diversity, 2, 4
responsive readings, 102
retreat, 52–54
rhythms, 91–92
rituals
    Advent, 81–85, 121–25
    delivery angels, 104–5
    preparation, 103
    reclaiming, 79–81
    still life tableaus, 63–75

sacred space, 56–61
Schleiermacher, Friedrich, 19
science and faith experience, 45–50
secondary theology, 18–19
sensory experiences, 89–90
sermons, 10–14
seven deadly sins, 32–33
shared ritual, 103
spirit objects and animals, 62
spiritual experiences, 9–10, 28, 44, 62, 92–94
Stanfield, Burns, 10
Steinbeck, John, 61–62
still life tableaus, 63–75
storytelling, 76–79, 90
symbols
    as the artwork of belief, 56, 61–62, 64–67
    as definition of sacred space, 56–57
    God-encounter, 64
    interpretation of, 63–64
    participation, 60–61
    rituals, 70–75
    as unintended markers of sacred space, 57–59
    as windows to seeing God, 67–70, 71–74

Index

technical deacons, 108
technology, 98–110
testimonies, 88–89
Thandeka, 95n1
Thanksgiving prayer, 119–20
theological interpretation and appropriation, 26n3
theological terms, 29–34
Thinking Through Our Faith (Grant), 26n3
Tillich, Paul, 26n4
transformative spiritual experiences, 18, 44, 62, 92–94
transformative worship, 6–7

United Church of Christ, 1, 4–6, 38, 42, 105

Vermont Conference of the United Church of Christ, 88
virtual worship, 98–110
visual displays, 62, 63–75, 89, 103, 104

walking music, 49, 84
weekly liturgy, 37–38
Wilson, Ralph F., 15–16
windows to the world, 105
worship experience. *See also* language of worship; rituals; symbols
   age-old refrains, 22–24
   Benediction, 111–13
   centering meditation, 35–36
   children, 4–5, 7, 12, 49
   Christian traditions, 80–81
   as emotional, 9–10, 14–18, 46–47, 69–70, 92–97
   essential gospel, 40–41
   God-encounters, 56, 93, 95, 99, 103, 109, 113
   images in, 103
   intellect, 11, 46
   liturgical mapping, 95–97
   music, 42–54
   order of worship, 94–95
   personal sharing, 104
   primary theology, 18–20
   sacred space, 56–61
   science, 45–50
   sensory experience, 89–90
   still life tableaus, 63–75
   storytelling, 90
   technology, 98–110
   ulterior motives, 11–12
   virtual worship, 98–110
   worship space, 99–100
worship liturgy, 4–6
worship planning and leadership
   Benediction, 111–13
   emotional flow of worship, 92–97
   essential gospel, 41
   focus, 13–14
   hybrid worship, 109–10
   Jesus story, 78
   language of worship, 85–87
   liturgical mapping, 95–97
   music, 50, 51–54
   order of worship, 94–95
   pastoral roles, 108
   pitfalls, 13
   reclaiming ritual, 79–81
   resources to refresh liturgies, 34
   transformative spiritual experiences, 43–44
   virtual worship, 98–110
   visual displays, 62

Zoom Meetings, 100–101, 104, 106–8

www.ingramcontent.com/pod-product-compliance
Lightning Source LLC
Chambersburg PA
CBHW050828160426
43192CB00010B/1942